Hi Karlee,
Bob Burke
2007

Karlee,
Play on!
Dick

FOR ALL *GOOD* SPORTS

A HISTORY OF THE OKLAHOMA CITY ALL SPORTS ASSOCIATION

BY BOB BURKE AND DICK DUGAN
FOREWORD BY MICK CORNETT

Oklahoma Horizons Series

SERIES EDITOR: GINI MOORE CAMPBELL
ASSOCIATE EDITOR: ERIC DABNEY

OKLAHOMA HERITAGE ASSOCIATION
OKLAHOMA CITY

FOR ALL *Good Sports*

ISBN   10-digit 1-885596-62-6
          13-digit 978-1-885596-62-8

Library of Congress Catalog Number
          2007936203

Designed by Kris Vculek

Printed by Bart Baker Group, LLC &
Jostens, Inc.- 405.503.3207

OKLAHOMA HERITAGE ASSOCIATION

OKLAHOMA CITY

1.888.501.2059

www.oklahomaheritage.com

2007 OKLAHOMA HERITAGE ASSOCIATION

THIS BOOK MADE POSSIBLE BY CONTRIBUTIONS FROM:

A Cross Ranch Ltd.
Big 12 Conference
Oklahoma City Centennial
   Committee
John A. Philbin
The Oklahoman
   & NewsOK.com

AT&T-Oklahoma
Donald G. Douglas
Midwest Wrecking Company
Smith, Carney & Co., CPA
Kenneth W. Whittington, M.D.

Bogert Energy
Clyde Riggs Construction
Dr. Don Halverstadt
First United Bank, Derek B. Gill
Johnson & Associates, Inc.
Kansas City Blues BBQ-
   Ground Floor Café-The Lunch Box
D.E. "Rick" Lippert, Jr. / Lippert
   Brothers, Inc.
Ken and Craig McAlister
Stephen H. McDonald &
   Associates, Inc.
In Memory of Thurman R. Medley
Mutual Assurance Administrators, Inc.
Oklahoma Employees Credit Union
Charles Susan
Jack R. Thompson

Arrowhead Energy, Inc.
Marty Askins
BancFirst
Dick J. Beshear
Mike and Barbara Bohrofen
Matt Bown
Bob Butcher
Ben & Terry Byers in memory of
   Gene & Margaret Cheatham
James E. Cheatham, Jr., MD
Glenn Ashmore, DDS / Dental Depot
David B. Duck
Dick and Dee Dugan
Dr. Robert S. Ellis
Dr. Teresa Folger
Walter Gillispie
Joan R. Gable
H&H Masonry Contractors, Inc.
Joan B. Hambrick
Horne & Company, P.C.
Jackie Cooper BMW-Mini
Marolyn Pryor Realtors
Jack Moncrief
Moser Law Office
F. Todd Naifeh

Shannon and Mark Nance
Oklahoma Tank Lines
Ken Culver, Pension Solutions
Chris Pierce
Professional Insurors Agency, LLC
John & Lindy Ritz
Roger Hicks & Associates Group
   Insurance, Inc.
Cecil and Linda Smith
Lee Allan Smith
Southwest Trailers & Equipment
Bob Stephenson
The Sheraton Oklahoma City Hotel
Terry Neese Personnel Services
R. Dale Vaughn
J. Blake Wade
Mark and Carol Williams
Gaylan D. Yates, MD

4

ACKNOWLEDGMENTS

It took cooperation from many people to make this book happen. Book committee chairman Dick Dugan was assisted by members of his committee, Mark Williams, Ben Byers, and Daniel Medley, and All Sports Association staff members Wilma Goodin, Jordan Satarawala, Emily Bone, and Ashlee Nichelson.

Thanks to Stefanie Carmack for her professional expertise, extensive research, and material organization. We are also thankful to Gini Campbell, director of publications for the Oklahoma Heritage Association, and Eric Dabney for their editing of the material. Kris Vculek did a superb job in designing the cover and interior of the book.

Appreciation is due Linda Lynn, Melissa Hafer, Mary Phillips, Robin Davison, and Billie Harry of *The Oklahoman,* and Mike Coker for editorial assistance and selection of photographs.

The Authors • 2007

Stanley Draper, Jr. was director of the Oklahoma City All Sports Association for 42 years. *Courtesy Oklahoma Publishing Company.*

DEDICATION

The officers, staff, and members of the board of the Oklahoma City All Sports Association dedicate this history to Stanley Draper, Jr., who for 42 years served as the ASA Executive Director.

We heartily agree with a tribute to Stanley in *The Oklahoman* after his death on May 27, 2006.

Stanley Draper Jr. died Saturday during the Big 12 baseball tournament and a few days before the Women's College World Series opened.

Fitting. Few people have done more for Oklahoma City sports than did Draper in his 42 years as executive director of the All Sports Association.

OKC rides high these days, some nine months before the Big 12 basketball tournament makes its Oklahoma City debut. The Ford Center is a regular stop for the NCAA tournament, the NCAA Wrestling Championships were just at the Ford Center and big-time events have become the norm, not the exception. No single person is more responsible than Draper. From 1957 through 1999, he led the All Sports Association as an exemplary organization for working with local schools and national organizations in enticing events to Oklahoma City.

Cities much larger than OKC do not have an organization so efficient and so committed as the All Sports Association. Cities much smaller than OKC do not have the civic support in terms of volunteers and corporate involvement and government backing.

Stanley Draper, Jr. was the glue.

CONTENTS

FOREWORD

Oklahoma City Mayor Mick Cornett.

It is one of those thought provoking questions that will make you think. What would the history of sports be in Oklahoma City if not for the All Sports Association? The short answer is: "We don't know but we sure don't want to find out."

Since 1957 the All Sports Association has been Oklahoma City's ticket to the highest levels of athletic entertainment. From NCAA Championship events, to Professional Rodeo, to the Sooner State games and dozens of events in between, the All Sports Association always has been special to Oklahoma City. They've built a stadium, built traditions, and in a sense played a major part in the building of our urban renaissance. They are special to Oklahoma City's history. And because of that, they are special to me too.

You first think of the wonderful memories involving generations of sports fans who have enjoyed the All-College Basketball Tournament—the longest running tournament of its kind.

I was eleven years old and sitting high atop the State Fair Grounds Arena in 1969 when I watched 5' 9" Calvin Murphy earn Tournament MVP honors for Niagara. He hit a game-winning shot and dazzled Oklahoma City sports fans with his ball handling and ability to score points in bunches.

In 1974, I was 16 and old enough to drive myself downtown to sit in the Myriad and watch 7' 1" Robert Parish claim MVP honors for Centenary. He was the tallest person I had ever seen!

I was sitting on the floor literally, and a member of the media in 1983 when Oklahoma's Wayman Tisdale scored 61 points against Texas-San Antonio. I'll never forget it.

And I was courtside at the Ford Center in 2005 when I sat as the city's mayor cheering both Oklahoma and Oklahoma State to victory.

Just one person's story, but so emblematic of the depth of the All Sports Association on our community.

Since 1929 the All-College has been our very own. Dateline: Oklahoma City. We were literally the only game in town, and not just our town but everyone's. It's been special to three generations. A December Christmas present in which the best and brightest dropped by our fair city to slug it out on a national stage.

The history is long and impressive, great names from great games: Elgin Baylor and Bob Lanier; Bill Russell and Nate Thurmond; Pete Maravich and Calvin Murphy; Robert Parish and Winford Boynes; Karl Malone, Wayman Tisdale, and Mookie Blaylock; Mr. Iba, Ray Meyer, Abe Lemons, Eddie Sutton, and Billy Tubbs.

It's hard to find an aging baby boomer who doesn't remember going to the Municipal Auditorium to watch hoops on the stage. Originally a 32-team tournament, and then an eight-team double-elimination affair, there were games all day for what seemed like weeks. It wasn't uncommon to be watching future NBA stars playing in the matinee in what was heaven on earth for kids out of school for the holidays.

But as sports in our country and city changed, so did the All-College. What was born out of it some 50 years ago was the Oklahoma City All Sports Association, which became among the first organization of its kind for any major city in America.

Where once it was the All-College Tournament that was special, it has since become the All Sports Association that shines a light both on and in our community.

The All Sports mission statement is to: secure, promote, create, execute and host quality, family oriented, amateur sporting events in the state of Oklahoma, thus enhancing the quality of life and creating a positive economic impact while producing national awareness.

Ladies and gentlemen — mission accomplished. Through the organized work of the All Sports Association, Oklahoma City has become the collegiate championship headquarters of the world, hosting 28 NCAA Championships, hundreds of conference championships, numerous non-championship national tournaments, and various national events to date. The results have been unequaled national attention, hundreds of millions of dollars in economic impact, and a national reputation as a friendly and welcoming host in a vibrant and flourishing city.

And to our own, the All Sports Association Sooner State Games and other grassroots amateur athletic endeavors bring a level of competition and participation to thousands of Oklahoma athletes throughout the state yearly.

For some, this book will provide a coffee table full of memories and for others a reference to history they can now share. For all it will provide a reminder and recognition of the board members, members, corporate sponsors, and volunteers whose time, leadership, and talent have made the All Sports Association our city's leading ambassador for the past half century.

I've played several roles throughout my life in Oklahoma City: journalist, businessman, mayor, father, and son. And in all of those roles, I have benefited from the wonderful work of the men and women who roll up their sleeves and work endlessly to create a better city through sports. We have been well served. To the futuristic city leaders of 1957 who dreamed up the idea of the All Sports Association, I raise a city's collective glass for a multi-generational toast. Well done. And here's to another great 50 years.

Mick Cornett
Mayor of Oklahoma City • 2007

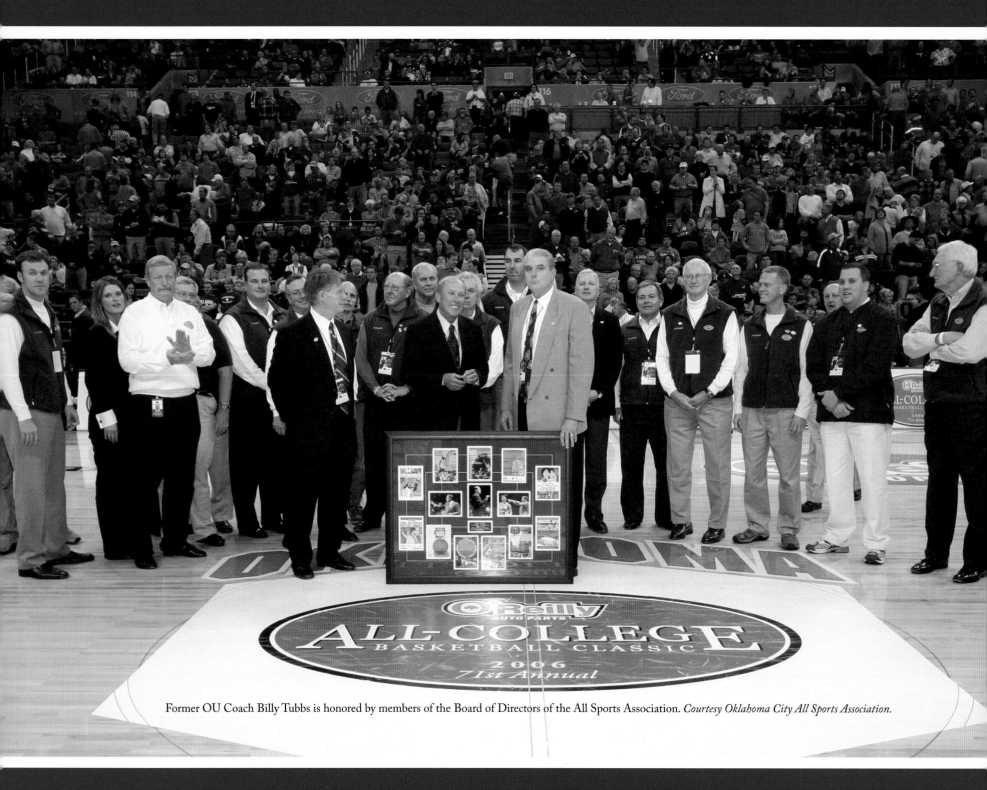

Former OU Coach Billy Tubbs is honored by members of the Board of Directors of the All Sports Association. *Courtesy Oklahoma City All Sports Association.*

THE ALL-COLLEGE TOURNAMENT

The nation's oldest holiday college basketball tournament began in a most informal manner 21 years before the formation of the Oklahoma City All Sports Association. In 1936, Oklahoma A & M Coach Henry P. Iba and Bus Ham, sports editor of *The Daily Oklahoman*, conceived the idea for a college basketball tournament for Oklahoma City for the week between Christmas and New Year's Day.

What Iba and Ham realized was that college teams were having difficulty getting good teams to play them before Christmas. Coaches were eager for competition to prepare their teams for league play after the first of the year. Iba and Ham put together a small committee of primarily sportswriters for the newspaper to invite teams and promise to pay mileage. The small stipend certainly assured participating teams of losing money, but they needed competition.

Coaches were quick to respond to the invitations. Even though the first field of 16 teams was not shaped until a week before the tournament, the prospect of top-notch college basketball games in Oklahoma City created a buzz among sports fans and city fathers.

The first All-College Tournament began on December 30, 1936. Ham wrote in his morning column in *The Daily Oklahoman:*

Sixteen of the finest teams in the southwest will dribble and dunk on the Classen High School court this afternoon and night, introducing the newest winter sports extravaganza, the all-college basketball tournament.

This event was conceived for the sole purpose of reviving a vigorous, exhilarating sport that once hung them over the balconies over all Oklahoma, but dropped pretty low in public favor a few years ago.

Here it is, gentlemen, this four-day dribble derby. Basketball has picked itself up and come bouncing back to popularity in other parts of the nation, and it will here too.

The beneficiary of the first All-College Tournament was the Milk and Ice Fund. The Oklahoma Publishing Company had sponsored many athletic events over the years to benefit the fund that provided money to buy milk and ice for disadvantaged children and families. Because of the charity nature of the first tournament, Ham wrote in his column, "Oh, yes, about the passes. There are not to be any. So please do not insist on shouldering your way past the gatekeeper…Most persons do not mind paying to see good entertainment when they know that the others there also paid to get in. Rest assured that only the players, coaches, officials, and hired help will be in free."

Ham wanted the tournament games to be entertaining. He asked the officials, Earl Jones, Jim Lookabaugh, Clarence Breithaupt, and James "Skimmer" Miller, to hold the whistle-blowing to a minimum, although Ham pointed out, "the plays will be called hard at first so that the tournament will not be sullied by avoidable roughness."

Ham and his staff convinced the W.L. Buck Sporting Goods Company to provide the trophy to the most valuable player in the four-day competition. Ham did not sleep much in the final days before the tournament kicked off. The final field of 16 teams contained a dozen teams from Oklahoma.

At 2:00 p.m. on December 30, the first tournament game tipped off at Classen High School. The game featured the Oklahoma City University (OCU) Goldbugs, long before they were called the Chiefs and now the Stars, and Phillips University. Center Red Bryan and forward Chester Bryan led the Goldbugs to a 49-35 win.

Other first-round games were played at Classen and Central high schools. Northwestern Oklahoma State College beat Panhandle A & M College; the University of Tulsa upended Oklahoma Baptist University; Baylor University bombed Southwestern Oklahoma Teachers College; Central State Teachers College beat West Texas State College; Southwestern Kansas State College beat Southeastern Oklahoma State College; Texas Tech beat East Central Oklahoma State College; and Oklahoma A & M swamped Northeastern Oklahoma State College.

Oklahoma A & M basketball coach Henry P. Iba, one of the founders of the All-College Tournament, stands proudly with his player, A.D. Bennett, who won the Most Valuable Player trophy at the 1948 All-College Tournament. *Courtesy Oklahoma Publishing Company.*

The starting five of the Oklahoma A & M Aggies as they practiced for the eighth annual All-College Tournament in December, 1943. Clockwise from Bob Kurland, No. 54, Jack Hance, Danny Doyle, Tom Jaquet, and Floyd Burdette. *Courtesy Oklahoma Publishing Company.*

Oklahoma A & M's Don Johnson takes off with a shot toward the basket during a win over the University of Idaho in the 1951 All-College. *Courtesy Oklahoma Publishing Company.*

Future legendary basketball coach Don Haskins goes flying through the air before hitting a layup for Oklahoma A & M in 1953. *Courtesy Oklahoma Publishing Company.*

Later, *Oklahoman* sportswriter Frank Boggs wrote about the first tournament field, "Come to think of it—with all the Northeasterns and Southwesterns and East Centrals and the like—a man probably needed a compass more than he did a program to keep up with the action."

OCU and Oklahoma A & M were bracketed to meet in the second night of the tournament. Goldbugs Coach Melvin Binford was not worried about facing Coach Iba's Aggies. Binford said, "Don't think we are crying about meeting the Aggies. My kids want them. We may take them."

Famous last words! The Aggies beat OCU 39-27. Texas Tech, Baylor, and Tulsa advanced along with the Aggies to the semifinals. The Aggies held Texas Tech to just 19 points to their 38, and earned a spot in the first All-College finals with Tulsa, that had won 26-23 over Baylor.

The first championship game was over early. At halftime, A & M led 22-9. The final score was 40-17 with 10 Aggies scoring from Iba's cleared bench. In four tournament games, A & M scored 158 points.

Aggies Dick Krueger and Merle Rousey, Tulsa's Robert Jones and Carl Brown, and Baylor's Hubert Kirkpatrick were named to the first all-tournament team. Jones won the Most Valuable Player Award. Kirkpatrick won the individual scoring title. He scored 49 points in four games, slightly more than 12 points a game—a huge effort in the slow pace of 1936 college basketball.

High-stepping Roger Holloway of Oklahoma City University controls the ball while surrounded by teammates Cecil Magana, left, and Lyndon Lee, right, and the University of Tulsa's Dick Courter and Bob Patterson, No. 31. *Courtesy Oklahoma Publishing Company.*

The new tournament was well received and fans believed they had received their money's worth. A reserved seat was 75 cents, general admission was 40 cents, and students could see a game for a quarter.

The initial All-College crowd was not just fans from Oklahoma City and supporters of the teams playing in the tournament. Fourteen members of the 29th Infantry team from Fort Sill, Oklahoma, watched the games. Lieutenant T. R. Stoughton, the team's coach, said, "We thought we would come up to see how big-time college ball is played, get some pointers, then go back home and beat everybody!"

The first All-College actually lost $1,700, but coaches liked the play as a laboratory in which they experimented for conference games later in the season. With the initial success, the tournament committee invited 22 teams for 1937, with the final game to be played at Municipal Auditorium, the largest venue in Oklahoma City.

Oklahoma A & M won its second consecutive All-College title before a paying crowd of nearly 5,000 fans. Financial success had arrived for the tournament. The Aggies played for the championship against the Moundbuilders of Southwestern Kansas State College.

One of the brightest college prospects of the season was Southwestern's Lloyd Tucker. However, Tucker fouled out at halftime with just six points and his team leading by one point. Without Tucker, Southwestern was crippled. The Aggies won the game 26-22, although Tucker was the unanimous choice as the most valuable player of the tournament and scored 80 points in five games. The single-game scoring record was surpassed by F. M. Sachse who scored 27 points for Texas Tech in its win over Oklahoma Baptist University. Tech also set a new team scoring record—54 points—in the same game.

The Aggies were favored to win the third All-College in 1938. Of the 447 players on the rosters of the expanded field of 32 teams, only five were taller than 6'6". First-round games were played at Central and Classen high schools and the Municipal Auditorium. One game was even played at the high school gymnasium in Comanche, Oklahoma. Central Oklahoma and Texas Christian University (TCU) met in Comanche in southern Oklahoma, about halfway between Edmond and Fort Worth, Texas. C. B. Speegle scored 22 points and Central State whipped TCU 52-45.

The 1938 tournament featured a stunning upset. Oklahoma A & M lost in the semifinals at Classen High School before a crowd of 2,500 to the state college team from Warrensburg, Missouri, 31-23. Warrensburg then beat the University of Texas, 33-25, in the All-College Tournament championship game.

A humorous moment occurred during the 1938 classic. Southeastern Oklahoma Coach Bloomer Sullivan opened the tournament souvenir program and found the school's publicity man, Pete Alston, listed as the coach. Alston obviously had sent the Southeastern roster to tournament headquarters and a secretary assumed he was the coach. Sullivan told a reporter, "Well I'll be danged! It's hard enough to hang onto a coaching job these days without having your own publicity writer run under you!"

As the 1940s appeared, college basketball saw massive changes in taller players and higher scoring offenses. In 1941, West Texas State came to the tournament averaging 72 points a game with Charles Halbert, at 6'10", dubbed the tallest man in basketball. The starters for West Texas averaged 6'6", towering above most teams they played. Frank Boggs wrote, "There was one other thing the 1941 West Texas State team had going: those tall guys were athletes. They could shoot and they could run and they knew what basketball was about."

The Buffaloes were hot. In the opening round they beat East Central Oklahoma 70-37. In a tougher second game, West Texas beat Oklahoma A & M 73-31.

That was the only tournament that Loyd Ball of Rocky, Oklahoma, has not attended in the 71-year history of the All-College. There was a blizzard between Rocky and Oklahoma City. However, Ball closely listened to his radio for results of the games. He said, "I was already hooked on the incredible action I saw each year at the All-College. I had always liked basketball, both as a player and as a referee, but the level of competition I saw at the All-College was better than anything in this part of the country. I saw both great players and legendary coaches."

Loyd Ball of Rocky, Oklahoma, is honored during the 2005 All-College. Board members Mark Williams, left, and Mike Bohrofen presented an award to Ball for attending all but one of the tournaments in its 71-year history. *Courtesy Oklahoma City All Sports Association*

The All-College continued to draw decent crowds throughout the 1940s and early 1950s. However, the large number of teams invited to the tournament increased costs to the point that officials began considering the idea of canceling the tournament, or severely limiting the number of teams. It was literally a year-to-year situation. A few businessmen would buy large advertisements in the souvenir program to provide adequate money to hold out hope for the life of the tournament.

In 1954, Oklahoma basketball fans were treated to one of the great individual performances in college basketball. The University of San Francisco (USF) came to town with a 4-1 record—its only loss to UCLA. Local fans and sportswriters knew very little about the Dons except for word from the West Coast about a 6'9" center, Bill Russell, who averaged 24 points a game in his first five contests that season. There was also a rumor Russell was an incredible rebounder.

Russell's teammates were no slouches, including K. C. Jones, a 6'1" guard. In the opening game, USF met unbeaten Wichita State University. In the first seven minutes, USF ran up a 25-3 lead. Wichita called time out. Their players' faces had silly grins, not believing what they were seeing from the San Francisco team. The final score was 94-75.

In the semifinal game against OCU, San Francisco rushed to a 40-17 lead on its way to a 75-51 win. Russell scored 25 points and gathered 21 rebounds. In the championship game, San Francisco pounded George Washington University 73-57. Russell had 30 rebounds to go with his 23 points. There was no doubt among sportswriters who named him the most valuable player of the tournament. John Cronley, who covered the tournament for *The Daily Oklahoman,* wrote, "If the springy, nimble, and graceful Californian isn't sure pop All-American caliber, then the crowds here were badly misled and the young man must have been miles over his head."

CHAMPION FANS

Loyd Stout of Cherokee, Oklahoma, has been attending the All-College Tournament since 1948. His trip to Oklahoma City in 1955 was especially memorable. On December 29, Loyd and his girlfriend, Martha, left the All-College between games, got married, and returned for the rest of the action. Loyd always has insisted that it was Martha's idea to find someone to marry them while in Oklahoma City.

The young couple was unable to find a best man or have any family members present for the ceremony. When they returned to their seats after the wedding, all dressed up, the fans on either side did not believe their story. However, the fans were made believers the following day when the newspaper account of the wedding was published.

Martha and Loyd Stout. *Courtesy Oklahoma City All Sports Association.*

This photograph appeared in the local newspaper in Cherokee, Oklahoma, showing the banner that friends of Loyd and Martha Stout produced at the All-College Tournament in 2004 to celebrate the Stouts' 48th wedding anniversary. *Courtesy Oklahoma City All Sports Association.*

Fans are the ultimate beneficiary of the hard work of staff, officers, board members, interns, and volunteers of the All Sports Association.
Courtesy of the Oklahoma City All Sports Association.

SAVING THE ALL-COLLEGE

Without the All Sports Association, the All-College Tournament would have been buried in a lonely grave years ago.
FRANK BOGGS

After the 1956 tournament, the Oklahoma Publishing Company, which had sponsored the All-College since 1936 as a charity event for the Milk and Ice Fund, decided to get out of the promotion business. Newspaper officials informed city leaders that if the tournament was to continue, someone else needed to take its place as the sponsor.

The Sports and Recreation Committee of the Oklahoma City Chamber of Commerce held a quick meeting. Business and civic leaders recognized that the All-College was good for the city and should be continued.

On January 23, 1957, the Oklahoma City All Sports Association (ASA) was created as a non-profit Oklahoma corporation with 41 volunteer board members. The founding documents describe the purpose of the new group as sponsoring, promoting, financing, and maintaining the All-College Tournament and fostering and encouraging participation and spectator interest in all athletic and sports events in the Oklahoma City area.

Five days later, at a meeting held at the Oklahoma City Chamber of Commerce offices in the Skirvin Tower Hotel, E. L. "Jim" Roederer, a recently-arrived insurance agent from Iowa, was elected as the first president of ASA; Thurman Medley and C. H. "Chuck" Simpson were chosen as vice presidents; Theron Elder was elected secretary-treasurer; and

Stanley Draper, Jr., was named executive secretary to run the day-to-day operations of the infant organization.

The ASA went on the offensive to convince the best possible eight teams in the region to take part in the 1957 tournament slated for the week after Christmas at the Municipal Auditorium. On February 4, it was announced that each team would, for the first time, receive a $2,000 guarantee and an increased travel allowance. The previous season, after expenses were deducted, each team received less than $1,000.

It was agreed that H. B. Lee chair the tournament committee for 1957 and that the first $3,000 profit would be kept by the ASA for the next year's tournament. All additional profit would be split among the eight schools and the ASA. The first board authorized Roederer and Lee to attend the NCAA tournament in Kansas City to help Jay Simon, *The Daily Oklahoman* sports editor and that year's tournament director, contact coaches and officials of interested schools.

For the next six months, Roederer pounded the pavement looking for new members. He announced a goal of 1,000 members. Meanwhile, the selection committee chose the eight schools for the first All-College under the sponsorship of the ASA—the University of San Francisco, Niagara

University, Idaho State University, Western Kentucky University, Tulane University, OCU, Denver University, and the University of Tulsa.

The 22nd All-College Tournament saw ticket prices rise to $1.50, $2.25, and $3.00. Afternoon sessions cost only $1.00 per person. Newspaper advertisements announced that advance tickets could be purchased at Veazey's Drug Store in downtown Oklahoma City.

A tournament breakfast was held at the Biltmore Hotel to give members of the ASA and their guests an opportunity to meet coaches of the eight schools. The breakfast was organized by Stanton Young and Harold "Scooter" Hines. Tickets for the breakfast were $2.00 each.

The first All-Queen was chosen. The lucky girl was Joan Hinz, a junior at OCU from Corn, Oklahoma. The princesses were Barbara Bates of Poteau, Oklahoma; Carolyn Whaley of Tulsa; and Judie Randolph of Oklahoma City.

The nation's top-scoring college team and two of the top-five defensive units made up the tournament field. Western Kentucky led the nation by scoring more than 95 points per game. San Francisco and Idaho State were third and fifth in allowing the fewest points per game. Coach Taps Gallagher's Niagara University team was among national leaders in both offense and defense. The unbeaten Purple Eagles were ninth in scoring and tenth in defense.

Two of the nation's top coaches also were featured in the 1957 All-College. Ed Biddle, coach of the Western Kentucky Hilltoppers, was first among active coaches with wins, at 667, and second in history only to Phog Allen of Kansas. San Francisco Coach Phil Woolpert was fresh off a 60-game winning streak spanning three seasons.

Number seven-ranked San Francisco beat OCU 60-45 in the championship game with a crowd of 4,200 looking on. It was the third

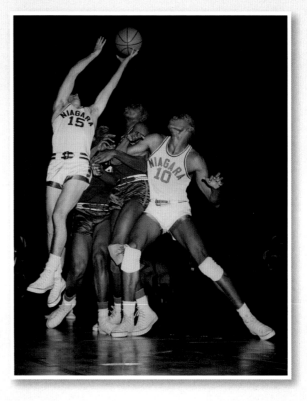

Going up for a shot against Utah State in the first round of the All-College in 1959 is Niagara University's Bill Roberts, No. 15, as Donald Jones, No. 10, jockeys Utah State's Cornell Green, left, and Tyler Wilben for rebounding position. Green is a member of the All-College Hall of Fame. *Courtesy Oklahoma Publishing Company.*

straight year that OCU had finished as runner-up in the tournament. Niagara beat Tulsa, 65-49, for third place.

When all the bills were paid for the first ASA-sponsored All-College, each board member had to make up $21.43 each. Not a bad investment for saving the tournament! In addition to being a financial success, more members were becoming part of the organization. By the end of 1957, ASA had 450 members.

Even though the ASA had been formed to save the All-College Tournament for Oklahoma City, the group soon began to branch out into other events. A Big Four doubleheader was launched at the Municipal Auditorium featuring OU, Tulsa, OCU, and OSU.

THE ALL SPORTS GUYS REALLY ARE

By Frank Boggs

When a guy takes his gal to a basketball game there is a man in a striped shirt who tosses a ball into the air, thereby triggering the start of one of the land's favorite pastimes—basketball watching. But he doesn't really realize the work that precedes the start of the action.

He might be aware some fellow is out there in a booth selling the tickets. And another guy tore it half in two before he'd walked another 20 feet. And another one looked at the half he had left and knew enough to tell him where to sit.

The spectator doesn't really notice, or care, that some guy with a wide broom has removed whatever collects on the shiny basketball floors; that someone saw that the heat was turned on early enough to keep winter outdoors; that somebody else popped the corn; that the guy in the concession stand didn't order the foot-long hot dogs until he'd made sure that the foot-long buns had been delivered; that the policemen were in the parking lot to assist with the arriving traffic; that the fellow behind the microphone had gathered the correct lineups; that the men who keep score were at their places; that the band members assembled an hour earlier to make sure the tuba wasn't sitting too close to the flute; and, perhaps, where the All-College Tournament is concerned, maybe he didn't even notice that the All Sports Association members were wearing their dark red coats and scurrying about to make sure all those other things were being handled.

During the 1958 All-College Tournament, 8,000 high school players from 250 schools in Oklahoma, Kansas, Arkansas, and Texas, attended afternoon sessions of the tournament compliments of Mr. and Mrs. Travis Kerr, owners of Roundtable, a highly successful race horse. For the next four years, the Kerrs provided tickets for high school players.

An added attraction for high school athletes and coaches at the 1958 All-College was a free basketball clinic at Municipal Auditorium. Abe Lemons and coaches of the other seven teams addressed the players and coaches, each with a different phase of the game.

Four youth basketball teams from the Oklahoma City area competed in what was billed as a Junior All-College. The teams—Junior Optimist, Lincoln Terrace Christian, Gilt Edge, and First Nazarene—played in the YMCA Junior League.

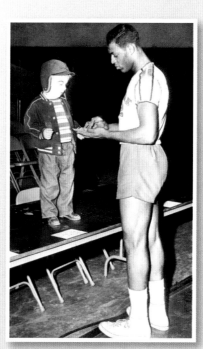

University of Seattle star and future National Basketball Association standout Elgin Baylor played in the 1958 All-College. *Courtesy Oklahoma Publishing Company.*

LEFT: Oklahoma City University Coach Abe Lemons, left, receives the second-place All-College trophy from All-College Queen Donna Waters in 1959. *Courtesy Oklahoma Publishing Company.*

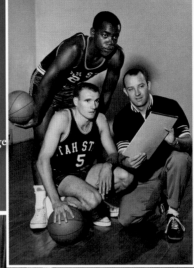

LEFT: In 1961, for the first time, both the most valuable player and scoring champion from the previous year played in the All-College. MVP Lanny Van Eman returned for Wichita University while scoring champion Cornell Green played for Utah State. Standing, Green, sitting, left to right, Don Holman and Utah State coach LaDell Andersen. *Courtesy Oklahoma Publishing Company.*

LEFT: In 1960, the All-College celebrated its silver anniversary. Utah State Coach Cecil Baker, right, and two of his players, Darnel Haney, left, and Tyler Wilbon, pose in the Biltmore Hotel lobby shortly after their arrival in Oklahoma City for the tournament. *Courtesy Oklahoma Publishing Company.*

Oklahoma City University's Hub Reed was a perennial favorite star of the All-College Tournament. *Courtesy Oklahoma Publishing Company.*

RIGHT: The All Sports Association reelected its officers in 1961. Left to right, Stanley Draper, Jr., executive secretary; Harold "Scooter" Hines, secretary treasurer; Jim Roederer, president; Roy Deal, second vice president; and Thurman Medley, first vice president. *Courtesy Oklahoma Publishing Company.*

TRULY AN ALL SPORTS ASSOCIATION

By Frank Boggs

Without the All Sports Association the current sports picture in Oklahoma City might consist of croquet in the backyard, a hot game of marbles when it wasn't too muddy, and jump-roping for girls who have not reached their eighth birthday before November 15. The ASA not only saved the All-College Tournament, and continued to upgrade the caliber of teams competing, but it also generated interest in nearly every other athletic venture.

Over the years the group of civic-minded men, none of whom realizes a penny's profit for his hours of work but all of whom stand to lose their own case in the event of an unsuccessful promotion, has sponsored darned near everything but jump-roping.

Bowling Green University's Nate Thurmond was a crowd pleaser on the court in the 1961 All-College. *Courtesy Oklahoma Publishing Company.*

ABOVE: In 1963, a packed crowd watched the All-College action. Note the old-fashioned supports for the backboard. *Courtesy Oklahoma Publishing Company.*

All-American Paul Silas played for Creighton University in the 1964 All-College. Silas went on to star in the National Basketball Association. *Courtesy Oklahoma Publishing Company.*

OCU ended a seven-year drought as All-College champion by beating Duquesne University in 1958. In inclement weather, 4,500 fans hailed the OCU victory and gave a tremendous ovation to Bud Shamaunt when he was named the tournament's most valuable player. OCU beat San Francisco and No. 1 seed, Xavier University, on its way to the championship game.

Significant developments to continue and enhance the success of the All-College have occurred in recent years. A classic two-team format was instituted in 2000. A title sponsorship was developed in 2001 with Touchstone Energy, a relationship which continued for four years.

A partnership with major impact, providing national television coverage and fielding of prominent teams, was formed with ESPN in 2002.

In 2005, O'Reilly Automotive was welcomed as title sponsor with a three-year agreement, and ESPN agreed to contract terms to continue to nationally televise the All-College games, giving unprecedented national publicity to Oklahoma City.

All Sports Association President Jim Roederer, left, is presented a bouquet of red roses from All Sports Queen Bonnie Bradshaw, a student at Oklahoma City University, in 1965. *Courtesy Oklahoma Publishing Company.*

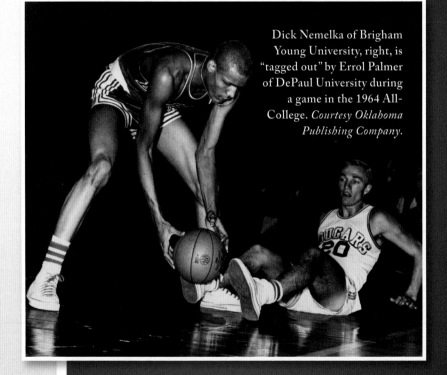

Dick Nemelka of Brigham Young University, right, is "tagged out" by Errol Palmer of DePaul University during a game in the 1964 All-College. *Courtesy Oklahoma Publishing Company.*

LEFT: Temple University's Joe Cromer finds room at the basket between Tom Storm, left, and Jack Gillespie of Wichita State University in 1966. *Courtesy Oklahoma Publishing Company.*

LEFT: Oklahoma City University Coach Abe Lemons, center, talks with his stars, Bud Koper, left, and Manuel Heusman, in 1961. *Courtesy Oklahoma Publishing Company.*

BELOW: Bob Lanier was an All-American for St. Bonaventure University and played in the 1968 All-College. *Courtesy Oklahoma Publishing Company.*

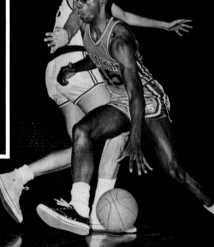

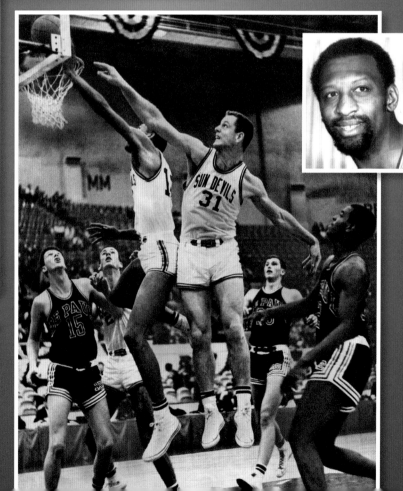

RIGHT: James Ware of Oklahoma City University drives toward the goal during the finals of the 1966 tournament. *Courtesy Oklahoma Publishing Company.*

RIGHT: Arizona State University center Bob Edwards goes up for a tip-in during a 93-59 loss in the battle for seventh place against DePaul University in the 1966 All-College. *Courtesy Oklahoma Publishing Company.*

Note the unique uniforms of the Oklahoma City University Chiefs as they played in the 1968 All-College Tournament. *Courtesy Oklahoma City All Sports Association.*

ABOVE: Memphis State University's 6'7" Fred Horton has the inside track on Tom Douthit of Arizona State University for this rebound in the 1969 tournament. *Courtesy Oklahoma Publishing Company.*

RIGHT: Duquesne University's Moe Barr hits a jumper over Louisiana State University's Rich Hickman in 1968. *Courtesy Oklahoma Publishing Company.*

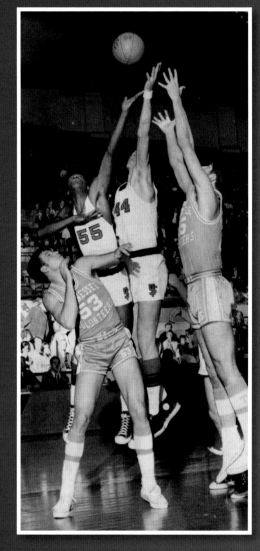

LEFT: Karl Lime of Brigham Young University strains as he tries to hook over the outstretched arm of Oklahoma City University's Willie Watson. The shot was blocked, but Watson was charged with a foul. Houston Thomas of the Chiefs looks on. The action occurred during the 1968 All-College. *Courtesy Oklahoma Publishing Company.*

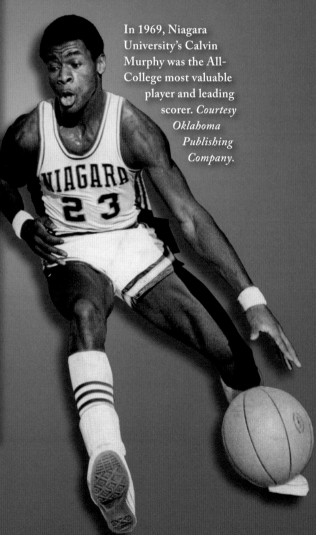

In 1969, Niagara University's Calvin Murphy was the All-College most valuable player and leading scorer. *Courtesy Oklahoma Publishing Company.*

ABOVE: Teams from all over the nation regularly played in the All-College Tournament. In 1969, the University of Tennessee played St. Francis College. St. Francis' Mike Copeland, No. 44, and Sam Slone out jump Tennessee's Don Campbell for a rebound. *Courtesy Oklahoma Publishing Company.*

RIGHT: All Sports Association Executive Director Stanley Draper, Jr., center, with two ASA presidents, Carl Grant, left, and Glenn Boyer. *Courtesy Oklahoma City All Sports Association.*

ABOVE: All Sports Association President Thurman Medley, left, pats Niagara University's Calvin Murphy on the back after being presented a special gold basketball to memorialize Murphy scoring his 2,000[th] point in his collegiate career. The mark came during the 1970 All-College. *Courtesy Oklahoma Publishing Company.*

Everybody is chasing the ball in the 1972 All-College. Mississippi State's Dean Hudson, left and Long Beach's Leonard Gray are going after the ball in different directions. *Courtesy Oklahoma Publishing Company.*

ABOVE: Oklahoma City University's Paul Hansen addresses an overflow crowd at the 1971 All-College kickoff banquet. To his left is All Sports Association President Carl Grant and Oklahoma City Mayor Patience Latting. *Courtesy Oklahoma City All Sports Association.*

Louisiana State University's Al Sanders tries to get away from the strong defense of Utah State's Ron Hatch during the All-College finals in 1970. Utah State won the game 97-81. *Courtesy Oklahoma Publishing Company.*

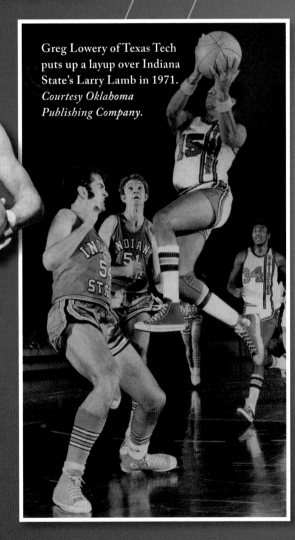

Greg Lowery of Texas Tech puts up a layup over Indiana State's Larry Lamb in 1971. *Courtesy Oklahoma Publishing Company.*

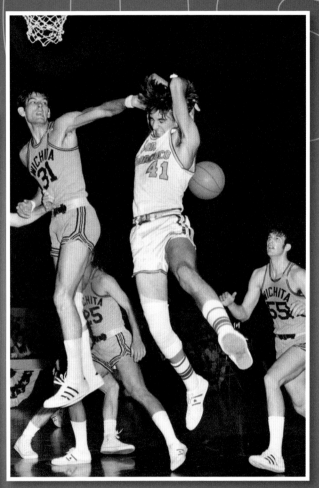

San Francisco University's Steve Ferreboeuf thought he had a rebound, but Wichita State University's Ron Soft changed that in a hurry during a first round All-College game in 1970. *Courtesy Oklahoma Publishing Company.*

Bowling Green's Dan Hipsher, No. 34, battles Robert Parish of Centenary College in a first-round contest of the All-College in December, 1975. *Courtesy Oklahoma Publishing Company.*

Oklahoma City University's Mike Tosee picks up an easy two points for the Chiefs in the 1972 All-College. *Courtesy Oklahoma Publishing Company.*

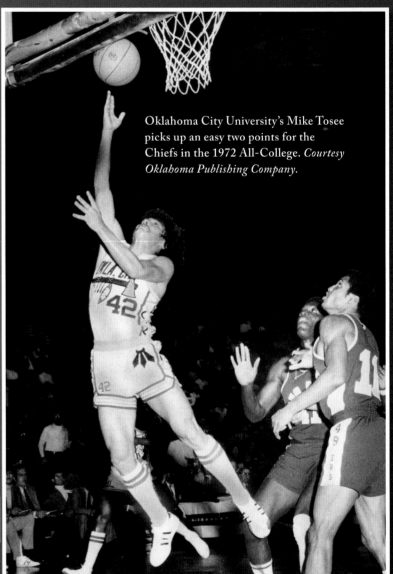

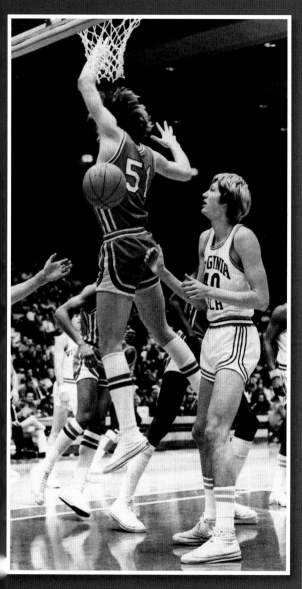

Kyle McKee, No. 40, of Virginia Tech watches David Marrs, No. 51, of the University of Houston go up for a rebound in the 1973 All-College. *Courtesy Oklahoma Publishing Company.*

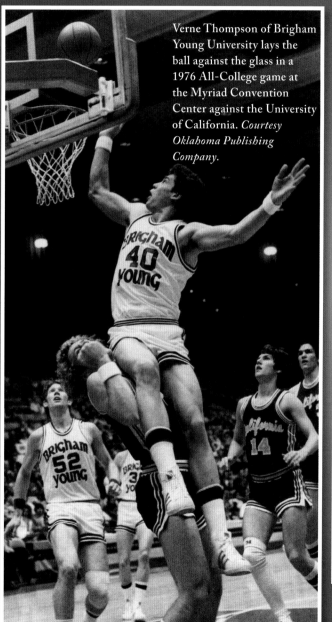

Verne Thompson of Brigham Young University lays the ball against the glass in a 1976 All-College game at the Myriad Convention Center against the University of California. *Courtesy Oklahoma Publishing Company.*

Oklahoma City University's David Will and two Webber State players watch the loose ball in the 1978 tournament. *Courtesy Oklahoma Publishing Company.*

ABOVE: In 1978, several former presidents of the All Sports Association posed for this photograph. Left to right, Executive Director Stanley Draper, Jr., Arnold Shelley, Thurman Medley, John Philbin, and Carl Grant. *Courtesy Oklahoma City All Sports Association.*

ABOVE: Oklahoma State University Coach Paul Hansen watches his players run the floor during the 1979 All-College. *Courtesy Oklahoma Publishing Company.*

ABOVE: The masters of the basketball coaching fraternity— Abe Lemons, left, and Henry P. Iba, meet at the All-College in 1980. *Courtesy Oklahoma Publishing Company.*

BELOW: In 1982, Oklahoma State University's Matt Clark was the most valuable player of the All-College. Two years earlier, he was the leading scorer in the holiday tournament. *Courtesy Oklahoma Publishing Company.*

BELOW: Manhattan's Sean Hall, No. 52, waits for the ball after Wayman Tisdale of the University of Oklahoma slams in a two-handed dunk during OU's rout of the Jaspers in the 1984 All-College Tournament. *Courtesy Oklahoma Publishing Company.*

ABOVE: All Sports Association President Carl Grant presents the championship trophy to the Oklahoma State University Cowboys in 1982. *Courtesy Oklahoma City All Sports Association*

The All Sports Association ticket application for the 1989 All-College Tournament. *Courtesy Oklahoma City All Sports Association.*

54th Annual
1935-1989
ALL-COLLEGE
BASKETBALL
TOURNAMENT
DECEMBER 29-30, 1989

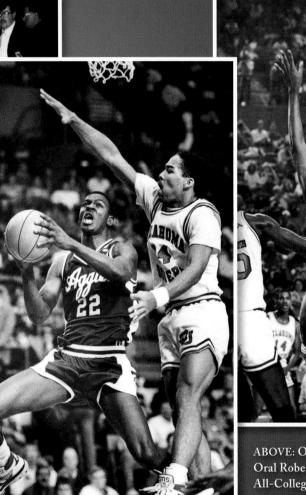

ABOVE: Presentation of post-tournament awards always is a fun time for All Sports Association staff and volunteers. This is the scene in 1989 at the Myriad Convention Center. *Courtesy Oklahoma Publishing Company.*

RIGHT: OU's Terrence Mullins goes one-on-one with Texas A & M's David Williams in the first round game in 1988. OU beat the Aggies 128-80 before a sellout Myriad crowd of 14,005. *Courtesy Oklahoma Publishing Company.*

ABOVE: OU center Stacey King puts up a shot over Oral Roberts University's Anthony Davis in a 1981 All-College Tournament game. *Courtesy Oklahoma Publishing Company.*

BELOW: Gene Cheatham, a founding board member who served on the board for 40 years, presents the MVP Award to Damon Patterson. *Courtesy Oklahoma Publishing Company.*

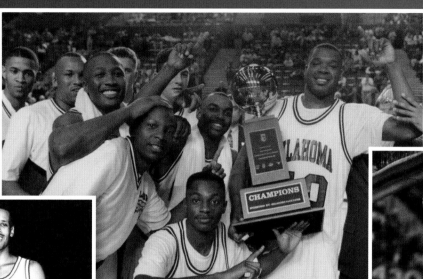

LEFT: A jubilant University of Oklahoma basketball team after winning the All-College championship in 1993. *Courtesy Oklahoma Publishing Company.*

RIGHT: The program cover for the 40th All-College in December, 1997. *Courtesy Oklahoma City All Sports Association.*

ABOVE: Tulsa University's Jeremy Rollo and OU's Ryan Minor battle for a rebound in the 1993 All-College. *Courtesy Oklahoma Publishing Company.*

Two former All-College stars, Scooter Hines, left, and Bob Kurland, visit at the Oklahoma Sports Hall of Fame Induction Ceremony in 2000. *Courtesy Scooter Hines family.*

BELOW: The 2006 All-College program cover. The University of Oklahoma beat the University of Tulsa in the championship. *Courtesy Oklahoma City All Sports Association.*

ABOVE: Fierce competition between players from the University of Oklahoma and West Virginia University symbolize the level of excitement fans enjoy at the annual O'Reilly All-College Basketball Classic. *Courtesy Oklahoma City All Sports Association.*

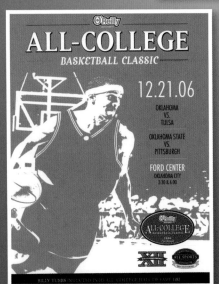

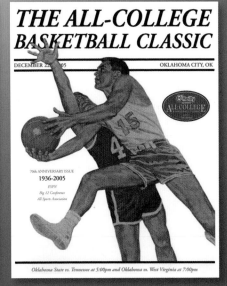

LEFT: The All-College Basketball Classic celebrated its 70th birthday in 2005. *Courtesy Oklahoma City All Sports Association.*

ABOVE RIGHT: An added attraction for kids at the annual O'Reilly All-College Basketball Classic is the Kids Basketball Adventure, an interactive basketball festival focused on family-oriented entertainment. Sporting good vendors, food, and entertainment lined the halls at the Cox Convention Center and kids had the opportunity to compete in basketball clinics. *Courtesy Oklahoma City All Sports Association.*

CELEBRATING **70 YEAR'S** OF ALL-COLLEGE TRADITION.

ABOVE: In the 70th anniversary program, an interesting presentation of All-College program covers met with fan approval. *Courtesy Oklahoma City All Sports Association.*

BELOW: Board members of the All Sports Association posed to welcome and thank O'Reilly Auto Parts for sponsoring the All-College Basketball Classic. *Courtesy Oklahoma City All Sports Association.*

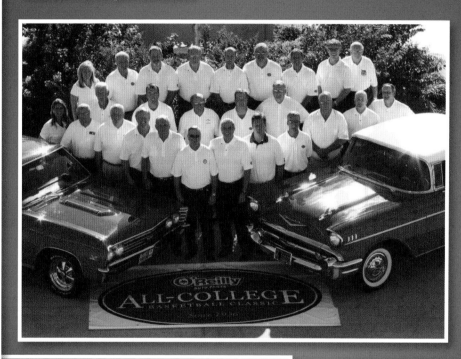

At the 2005 All-College banquet, left to right, board members Joe Groves, John Philbin, and Dr. Ken Whittington, and guest, Josh O'Brien of the Greater Oklahoma City Chamber of Commerce. *Courtesy Oklahoma City All Sports Association.*

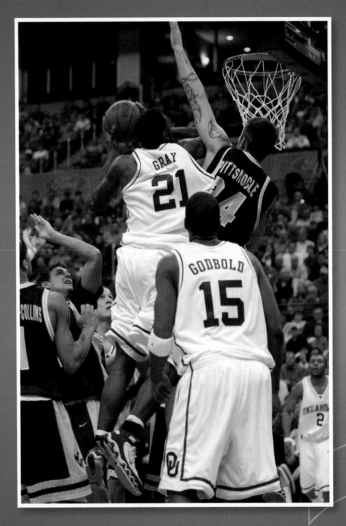

ABOVE: Sean Sutton makes his All-College debut as head coach of Oklahoma State University in the 2006 classic. *Courtesy Oklahoma City All Sports Association.*

RIGHT: University of Oklahoma freshman Kevin Bookout goes up against Michigan State University's Paul Davis in the January, 2005 All-College. *Courtesy Oklahoma City All Sports Association.*

West Virginia's Kevin Pittsnogle makes shooting tough for OU's tournament most valuable player Taj Gray in the 2005 All-College. *Courtesy Oklahoma City All Sports Association.*

BELOW: Oklahoma State University's JamesOn Curry in the 2006 All-College Classic. *Courtesy Oklahoma City All Sports Association.*

Gonzaga's Adam Morrison scores another three-pointer over Oklahoma State University's Daniel Bobik in the December, 2004 All-College. *Courtesy Oklahoma City All Sports Association.*

CLASSIC COLLECTION

CL 5

In 1980, basketball writers voted Bill Russell the greatest player in NBA history. The menacing 6-10 center helped guide the Boston Celtics to 11 NBA Championships in his 13 seasons (1956-69). He averaged 22.5 rebounds per game for his career, including 51 in one game in 1960. No man, in fact, has hauled down more boards in the NBA Playoffs (4,104). Though blocked shot statistics were not kept officially, it has been estimated that Russell swatted away 8 to 10 per game. Five times he was named League MVP, earning top honors in 1958, '61-63 and '65.

BILL RUSSELL

©1999 NBA PROPERTIES, INC. CREATED BY THE TOPPS COMPANY, INC.
TOPPS IS A REGISTERED TRADEMARK OF THE TOPPS COMPANY, INC.

Topps issued this commemorative trading card honoring Bill Russell for his championship career. Russell was inducted into the All-College Hall of Fame in 1971. *Courtesy Topps Company, Inc.*

THE ALL-COLLEGE HALL OF FAME

In 1967, the board of directors of the Oklahoma City All Sports Association voted to establish a Hall of Fame to honor players, coaches, and ASA volunteers and officers who helped make the All-College Tournament successful. The first inductee was Henry P. Iba. Legend has it that when the committee met to pick the first member of the Hall of Fame, it took members only seven seconds to agree upon Coach Iba.

HENRY P. IBA

"Mr. Iba" transcended greatness. The coach who helped originate the All-College Tournament also produced 11 tournament champions. His name became synonymous with the game of basketball.

Henry P. Iba was born in 1904 in Easton, Missouri. After high school, he played basketball at Westminster College of Missouri. In 1927 he became the basketball coach at Classen High School in Oklahoma City. He also played on amateur basketball teams for Sterling Milk and the Hillyard Shine Alls. In 1929, Iba left Classen to become head coach at Maryville Teachers College in Missouri. Later, he spent two years coaching the University of Colorado basketball team before moving to Oklahoma A & M College, now Oklahoma State University (OSU), in Stillwater in 1934.

Because of the Great Depression and a depressed athletic department budget at A & M, Iba coached both the basketball and baseball teams. He also became athletic director in 1935. As the baseball coach, he discovered the great Allie Reynolds who became a star pitcher for the Cleveland Indians and New York Yankees.

But it was basketball that would transform Iba from a tough, methodical coach into a legend. His Cowboys became the first team to win consecutive NCAA titles in 1945 and 1946. Iba was voted coach of the year in both seasons. He won 14 Missouri Valley Conference titles and closed his career in 1970 with a lifetime 767-338 record, placing him third best in NCAA Division I history. Under his leadership as athletic director, OSU won 19 national championships in five sports.

Iba's teams focused on ball control that featured weaving patterns and low scoring games. His "swinging gate" defense was applauded by many and is still occasionally seen in the college ranks.

Iba led the United States Olympic team to two gold medals, the only American basketball coach to do so. He also will be remembered as the coach of the 1972 Olympic team that lost to the Soviet Union in a controversial ending.

When Iba was inducted into the All-College Hall of Fame on December 27, 1968, ASA President Thurman Medley said, "This is the proudest moment in ASA history. Mr. Iba has become a legend in his own time. He's highly respected among his fellow men and by the people of the state of Oklahoma. Mr. Iba, we are glad to have been fortunate enough to have had a man like you come along in our time."

Mr. Iba's players are his greatest legacy. At the 1967 induction ceremony, Dick Krueger, one of the stars who led Iba's early teams, said, "Mr. Iba is by far the greatest man anyone could hope to come into contact with. He taught us everything we know—including how to behave in life."

Krueger said it was never easy to play for Coach Iba. "We worked hard," he said, "We started early and we stayed late. We'd work three times a day during Thanksgiving and get only a few days off at Christmas. We weren't wild. If you made one mistake, you didn't stay around."

Iba died in Stillwater on January 15, 1993. He is a member of the Oklahoma Hall of Fame, the Oklahoma Sports Hall of Fame, the Missouri Hall of Fame, the Helms Foundation All-Time Hall of Fame, and the Naismith Memorial Basketball Hall of Fame at Springfield, Massachusetts. Today, the Henry P. Iba Award is presented to the National Coach of the Year by the United States Basketball Writers Association.

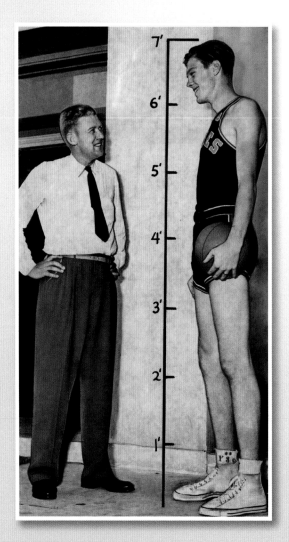

ROBERT "BOB" KURLAND

Robert Kurland, the first big man in college basketball, was born in Missouri in 1924. He lettered three years at Jennings High School and was state high jump champion in 1942. After high school he chose to play basketball at Oklahoma A & M because he could learn under Coach Iba and was promised a 35-cent-an-hour job in Stillwater, his books, and a bed that resembled the flight deck of an aircraft carrier.

At 7' Kurland overcame early teenage awkwardness to earn All-American honors in 1944, 1945, and 1946. In the later two years, when A & M won the national championship, the Associated Press voted Kurland the Most Outstanding Player of the Final Four. The Cowboys beat New York University in 1945 and the University of North Carolina in 1946 for the title. In 1946 Kurland led the nation in scoring with 19.5 points per game, remarkable for the low scoring era.

The first two members of the All-College Hall of Fame were Oklahoma State University basketball coach Henry P. Iba, left, and his seven-foot center, Bob Kurland. This photograph was taken when Kurland came to Oklahoma A & M in 1942. *Courtesy Oklahoma Publishing Company.*

Kurland was dominant in the three All-College Tournaments in which he played. He was selected as the most valuable player in two tournaments and made the all-tournament team all three years.

After he graduated from Oklahoma A & M, Kurland played six seasons for the Phillips 66ers, winning three national Amateur Athletic Union (AAU) championships. He also was a member of the 1948 and 1952 Olympic basketball squads that won the gold medal. He carried the American flag at the opening ceremony of the 1952 Olympics. In 1961 he was inducted into the Naismith Memorial Basketball Hall of Fame. He also is a member of the Helms Foundation Hall of Fame.

Kurland was the first All-College player enshrined in the All-College Hall of Fame. At the ceremonies preceding the 1968 tournament, Kurland said, "This truly warms the heart of an old warhorse." His coach, Henry P. Iba, told the audience about taking Kurland as a freshman to Madison Square Garden in New York City. Other coaches told Iba, "That boy will never play!" Iba and Kurland proved them wrong. Iba said, "He had great desire to be great."

Kurland had a successful business career as an executive with Phillips Petroleum Company.

BRUCE DRAKE

In 1969, Bruce Drake, the longtime University of Oklahoma basketball coach, became a member of the All-College Hall of Fame. Born in Texas in 1905, Drake learned to play basketball on the east side of Oklahoma City, firing at a basket nailed to the trunk of a cottonwood tree. In the same neighborhood was 6'6" Vic Holt who played at OU and later became president of the Goodyear Tire and Rubber Company.

Drake graduated from Oklahoma City's Central High School in 1925 and enrolled at the University of Oklahoma. He excelled in many sports at OU. He started on the basketball team, quarterbacked the OU football team for two seasons, and won the pole vault competition one year in the Big Six Conference. He vaulted 12'6" in a sweat suit.

Drake was captain of the OU basketball team in 1929 and was named to the Helms Foundation All-America team. He also was enshrined into the Helms Foundation Hall of Fame as a player that same year.

At OU, Drake was freshman coach from 1929 until he took over head coaching responsibilities in 1938. He had a 200-181 record through his retirement in 1955. Under Drake, the Sooners appeared in three NCAA tournaments, each

University of Oklahoma men's basketball coach, Bruce Drake. *Courtesy Oklahoma Publishing Company.*

time being eliminated by the eventual national champion. In 1947, OU lost in the NCAA finals to Holy Cross University and Bob Cousy. Drake won or tied for six conference championships in the Big Six and Big Seven.

Drake founded golf as a competitive sport at OU. His golfers once swept 33 consecutive dual meets. He also coached swimming for the Sooners.

After leaving OU, Drake coached the Air Force Academy team, was assistant coach for the American team in the 1956 Olympics, and became a member of the Helms Foundation Hall of Fame as a coach in 1961. He served as president of the National Basketball Coaches Association and chairman of the Joint Rules Committee of the United States and Canada.

Drake was induced into the Naismith Basketball Hall of Fame in 1971. The OU basketball practice facility was named in his honor after his death on December 4, 1983.

RAY MEYER

Ray Meyer, inducted into the All-College Hall of Fame in 1970, headed to college from Chicago's St. Patrick's High School wanting to be a social worker. After his high school team won the national championship in 1932, he played three years of collegiate basketball at the University of Notre Dame. He was team captain two years and played for Hall of Fame coach George Keogan. Meyer took part in a rare 20-20 tie game in 1935.

Meyer was successful as the men's basketball coach at DePaul University from 1942 until his retirement in 1984. At the time of his retirement, he was the fifth-winningest coach in NCAA Division I history with 724 wins. He guided the Blue Demons to 21 post-season appearances, had 37 winning seasons, twelve 20-win seasons, four Final Four appearances, and captured one National Invitation Tournament crown, the only post-season title for DePaul.

Meyer was national coach of the year in 1978 and 1979. He won the All-College Tournament in 1964. He died March 17, 2006.

Ray Meyer, left, receives a certificate honoring him as a member of the All-College Hall of Fame from Thurman Medley. *Courtesy Oklahoma Publishing Company.*

BILL RUSSELL

Russell, the cornerstone of the Boston Celtics dynasty in professional basketball, was inducted into the All-College Hall of Fame in 1971. He is a member of the All-College All-Time tournament team. He was born in Louisiana in 1934 but moved to California where he graduated from McClymonds High School in Oakland in 1952. He became an outstanding collegiate player at the University of San Francisco where he averaged more than 20 points and rebounds per game.

Russell led San Francisco to back-to-back NCAA championships in 1955 and 1956. He was the NCAA Tournament Most Outstanding Player in 1955 and the national player of the year in 1956. He also was a member of the American team that won the gold medal in the 1956 Olympics.

After college, Russell joined the Boston Celtics in 1956 and began one of basketball's greatest careers. In terms of leading his teams to championships, Russell is the National Basketball Association's (NBA) most honored player of all time. He won 11 championships in 13 seasons and many experts give him credit for raising defensive play in the NBA to a new level.

Bill Russell played in the All-College Tournament on his way to a legendary career in professional basketball. *Courtesy Oklahoma Publishing Company.*

Russell is one of only four players in history to win a national championship in his senior season in college and a NBA crown his rookie season. He was the first NBA player to average more than 20 rebounds per game for an entire season, a feat he accomplished 10 times in his 13 seasons. He ranks second only to Wilt Chamberlain in regular season total and average rebounds per game. His 51 rebounds in a single game trails only Chamberlain's record of 55.

In crunch time during playoffs, Russell leads in total rebounds with his average of 24.9 rebounds per game. He was the most valuable player of the NBA five times and won the MVP honor in the 1963 NBA All-Star game.

At the end of his playing career, Russell followed Red Auerbach as the coach of the Celtics, making him the first black head coach in any major professional sport in the United States. In eight seasons with Boston, Seattle, and Sacramento, Russell compiled a 341-290 record as an NBA coach.

He joined the elite in the Naismith Basketball Hall of Fame in 1975. In 1980, the Professional Basketball Writers Association of America declared Russell as the greatest player in the history of the NBA.

JAY SIMON

Also inducted into the All-College Hall of Fame in 1971 was Jay Simon, sports editor of *The Daily Oklahoman*. Simon was an incredible supporter of the All-College Tournament, making certain that the event received proper publicity and recognition. He served as tournament director in 1969.

Jay Simon looks at his certificate of induction into the All-College Hall of Fame. With Simon is All Sports Association President Thurman Medley, who later was inducted into the All-College Hall of Fame himself. *Courtesy Oklahoma Publishing Company.*

ABE LEMONS

In 1972, Oklahoma City University (OCU) basketball coach Abe Lemons was inducted into the All-College Hall of Fame. Lemons was born in 1922 in Walters, Oklahoma. After a stint in the Merchant Marine during World War II, he played basketball at OCU. He was named to the All-College Tournament team in 1949 and is a member of the All-College, All-Time team.

Sandwiched between his 25 years coaching at OCU, Lemons also was head basketball coach at Texas-Pan American University and the University of Texas. In 1977, he was president of the National Association of Basketball Coaches and was national coach of the year in 1978.

Lemons won the All-College three times, produced six All-American players, and led his team to six post-season appearances. He is a member of the Oklahoma Hall of Fame and the Oklahoma Sports Hall of Fame.

Even though Lemons is recognized as a great mentor of his players in teaching them how to live successful lives and to be men, he is best known for his funny quips, many in the heat of battle.

After he lost his final game by one point, leaving him one short of 600 career wins, Lemons said, "Damn referees! I'll miss them less than anybody!"

At halftime, when his center had grabbed only one rebound, Lemons said, "That's only one more rebound than a dead guy!"

Once when a group of supporters wanted him to leave his post, he told reporters, "They wanted to buy out my contract, but I couldn't make change for a $20, so they had to let me stay."

One afternoon appearing on national television, Lemons was being questioned about a bench decision by famous sportscaster Howard Cosell.

In 1970, Abe Lemons paid an extra $10 for a special license plate, proud of the fact he coached the Chiefs of Oklahoma City University. Unfortunately, "Chiefs" came spelled incorrectly, a mistake Abe had to live with for an entire year. *Courtesy Oklahoma Publishing Company.*

Lemons got mad and said, "Mister, you may be something in New York City, but you're nobody in Walters, Oklahoma!"

Lemons tried to recruit baseball hall-of-famer Johnny Bench of Binger, Oklahoma, to play basketball at OCU. At the end of Bench's all-star career, Lemons told him, "If you had come with me, you could be the principal of some high school by now!" On the value of practice, Lemons said, "One day of practice is like one day of clean living. It doesn't do you any good."

Other famous Lemons' quips are:

"Finish last in your league and they call you an idiot. Finish last in medical school and they call you doctor."

"Doctors bury their mistakes. Ours are still on scholarship!"

"I don't jog. When I die, I want to be sick."

"I never substitute just to substitute. I play my regulars. The only way a guy gets off the floor is if he dies."

Even as his health deteriorated Lemons never missed an All-College Tournament. He enjoyed being around great players and coaches and his friends who helped make the tournament successful each year. He died on September 2, 2002, in Oklahoma City.

JOHN "TAPS" GALLAGHER

John Gallagher was inducted into the All-College Hall of Fame in 1974. A graduate of St. John's University, Gallagher coached the Niagara University men's basketball team for 31 seasons. In his 26 winning seasons, he led his team to seven National Invitation Tournament berths. He won 11 Little Three championships and was the 1969 All-College Tournament champion. He had an overall record of 468-262. He died on February 7, 1982.

Utah State's Skyline Conference scoring champion in 1960 was Cornell Green. On his visit to the All-College he showed off his new streamlined haircut. *Courtesy Oklahoma Publishing Company.*

CORNELL GREEN

Named as one of the All-College All-Time greats, Cornell Green was inducted into the All-College Hall of Fame in 1975. He was born in 1940 in Oklahoma City and played college basketball at Utah State University. He made the All-College first tournament team three times, 1959-1961.

After college, Green played professional football for the Dallas Cowboys for 13 seasons. As a cornerback and safety, he was All-Pro six times. He was also a professional bowler for many years.

Green played in 168 games for the Cowboys, including 145 consecutive starts between 1962 and 1974. He led the team in interceptions four times. Coach Tom Landry said, "He had the athletic skills from basketball to become a fine defensive back. His only transition was playing a sport where you could tackle someone with the ball, and Cornell never had a problem dealing with that."

Following his retirement from the NFL, Green became a scout for the Cowboys and later the Denver Broncos.

STAN WATTS

Stan Watts, inducted into the All-College Hall of Fame in 1976, never had a losing record in 24 seasons as men's basketball coach at Brigham Young University (BYU). He was born in Utah in 1911 and graduated in 1938 from BYU. After a successful high school coaching career, he arrived as the freshman team coach at BYU in 1947. Two years later he became head basketball coach and began a 372-254 record. He won eight conference titles and appeared in 11 post-season tournaments. His team won the NIT championship in 1951 and 1965.

Watts coached disciplined teams that favored up-tempo play and showed relentless defensive pressure. He was the sixth coach to win 100 games in his first 500 games in NCAA Division I. He was president of the National Association of Basketball Coaches in 1970 and wrote the standard manual on the fast break offense, *Developing an Offensive Attack in Basketball*. He was enshrined into the Naismith Basketball Hall of Fame in 1986. He died on April 6, 2000.

JIM ROEDERER

Jim Roederer, first president of the All Sports Association, was inducted into the All-College Hall of Fame in 1977. He served nine years at the top of the ASA and was instrumental in bringing professional hockey and baseball to Oklahoma City. After several years without a minor league team, Roederer led the fight to convince the Houston major league baseball team to tab Oklahoma City for its top minor league farm team. He also headed the first promotion that resulted in the construction of the Myriad Convention Center in Oklahoma City, now the Cox Business Services Convention Center.

The credit for All Sports Association success in its first half-century must go to the organization's first president, Jim Roederer. He was a tireless civic worker and spent many hours promoting the All Sports Association. *Courtesy Oklahoma Publishing Company.*

THURMAN MEDLEY

In 1978, Thurman Medley, an Oklahoma City insurance agent, was inducted into the All-College Hall of Fame. He was born in Kiowa County, Oklahoma, in 1906 and was a charter member of the ASA. He was president of the organization from 1965 to 1978. For 22 years he was chairman of the tournament selection committee for the All-College Tournament.

In 1948, when Medley filled out a biographical sketch for *The Daily Oklahoman*, he listed his hobbies as "baseball, bowling, boys, and work." He dedicated his life to baseball, basketball, and boys.

Known as "Mr. Basketball," Medley was president of the Central Oklahoma American Legion baseball program from 1957 to 1976. In 1975 he was inducted into the Oklahoma Sports Hall of Fame. He died April 20, 1982.

Arnold Short was inducted into the All-College Hall of Fame in 1979. *Courtesy Oklahoma Publishing Company.*

ARNOLD SHORT

Arnold Short, a two-time All-American basketball player at Oklahoma City University, was inducted into the All-College Hall of Fame in 1979. He graduated from Weatherford, Oklahoma, High School before enrolling at OCU and launching a stellar collegiate basketball career. He is in the top ten in all-time OCU career scoring, led the Chiefs to the All-College championship in 1951, and was the All-College MVP in 1952. He holds the tournament record of hitting 23 free throws in a game against Baylor in 1954. He was named as one of the All-College All-Time Greats.

After college, he played for the Phillips 66ers

and was twice a first-team all-star in the National Industrial Basketball League. He was tennis coach at CU and head tennis pro at the Oklahoma City Tennis Center.

Short, a member of the OCU Hall of Fame, was the Chiefs' athletic director before becoming a Methodist minister.

PAUL HANSEN

Paul Hansen had the longest association with the All-College Tournament. He appeared as a player, assistant coach, and head coach in 28 tournaments. A graduate of Oklahoma City University, he was an assistant coach under Abe Lemons for 18 seasons before taking over the head-coaching responsibilities from 1974 to 1979. He was men's basketball coach at Oklahoma State University from 1980 to 1986 and also coached at the University of Science and Arts of Oklahoma at Chickasha, Oklahoma.

Hansen, who died in 1993, was one of the best-loved sports figures in Oklahoma. He was inducted into the All-College Hall of Fame in 1980.

After coaching the Oklahoma City University Chiefs, Hansen became head coach of the Oklahoma State University Cowboys. His wife, Carol, points to the new Cowboy pin when Hansen became the coach in Stillwater. *Courtesy Oklahoma Publishing Company.*

PETE MARAVICH

"Pistol Pete" Maravich learned his dazzling ballhandling, incredible shooting, and creative passing skills from his father, coach Press Maravich. Pete was born in 1947 in Pennsylvania and started for Louisiana State University (LSU) and four NBA teams. He is still the all-time leading NCAA scorer, averaging a staggering 44.2 points per game— without the benefit of the three-point line.

Maravich was inducted into the All-College Hall of Fame in 1987. He was MVP of the 1968 All-College and the leading scorer with 138 points in three games. At LSU he was an All-American for three seasons, was *The Sporting News* Player of the Year and the Naismith Award winner in 1970. As a professional player, he made the NBA All-Rookie team in 1971 and was a five-time all-star.

Pistol Pete owns many NCAA college basketball records—most field goals attempted and made, most free throws attempted and made, most games scoring at least 50 points (28), the single-season record for most points. In 1988, after Maravich's untimely death from a heart attack at age 40, LSU's home court was named the Maravich Assembly Center.

Pete was a unanimous choice as one of the All-College All-Time greats.

Pete Maravich, left, and former Oklahoma State University basketball coach Henry P. Iba, at a meeting of the All-College All-Time tournament team. *Courtesy Oklahoma Publishing Company.*

Glenn Boyer was president of the All Sports Association from 1983 to 1989, the year he was inducted into the All-College Hall of Fame. *Courtesy Oklahoma City All Sports Association.*

GLENN BOYER

For 11 years Glenn Boyer was chairman of the All-College Tournament selection committee. He was inducted into the All-College Hall of Fame in 1989 and was the fifth president of the ASA, serving from 1983 to 1989. He began service on the ASA board in 1975.

Boyer's first introduction to the All-College was as a player for Wichita State University in 1954. When he moved to Oklahoma City in the late 1960s, he came in contact with board member Jerry Bugg who was in his Sunday School class. Boyer became involved with ASA, joined the board, and eventually became president.

One of Boyer's fondest memories of the All-College Tournament is hosting Pete Maravich when he came to Oklahoma City to be inducted into the All-College Hall of Fame. Boyer remembered, "Pete spoke to the Fellowship of Christian Athletes and drew huge crowds everywhere we went. When I took him to the airport after the visit, he looked me in the eye and told me how special Oklahoma City had made him feel." Maravich died six days later.

STANLEY DRAPER, JR.

Born in 1923, Stanley Draper, Jr., the son of a pioneer Oklahoma City civic leader, attended Kemper Military Academy and the University of Oklahoma. After college he worked in the oil fields in Saudi Arabia before landing a job for the chamber of commerce in Corpus Christi, Texas.

In 1952 he joined the Oklahoma City Chamber of Commerce and assumed control of the chamber's sports and recreation committee in 1955. He was active in organizing the ASA in 1957 and became the organization's executive director, a role he magnificently filled for 42 years until his retirement in 1999.

Draper was a tireless promoter of Oklahoma City. He promoted and directed such events as the National Finals Rodeo, Aerospace America, Sooner State Games, 18 national NCAA tournaments, the National Aircraft Show, in addition to many one-time events. A charter member of the ASA, he was inducted into the All-College Hall of Fame in 1997. Two years later he became a member of the Oklahoma Sports Hall of Fame. He died on May 27, 2006.

WAYMAN TISDALE

The basketball player turned jazz guitarist was inducted into the All-College Hall of Fame in 2000. Wayman Tisdale was born in 1964 in Texas and attended Booker T. Washington High School in Tulsa and the University of Oklahoma. He is the OU career-scoring leader and was the first Sooner basketball player to have his number retired. He was a three-time All-American at OU and was a member of the Bob Knight-coached Olympic team in 1984 that won the gold medal.

Tisdale was the second overall pick in the 1985 NBA draft, going to the Indiana Pacers. In 12 professional seasons, he averaged more than 15 points and six rebounds per game. His best season was 1989-1990 for the Sacramento Kings when he averaged 22.3 points and 7.5 rebounds per game. He retired in 1997.

Prior to his retirement, Tisdale released his first jazz CD, *Power Forward*, in 1995. He was selected as one of the All-College All-Time Greats.

Tisdale had a momentous career playing in the All-College Tournament. He scored the most points, the most field goals, and had the most rebounds in a 1983 game against the University of Texas-San Antonio. He also holds the All-College record of total points and total field goals in a single tournament.

JOHN PHILBIN

John Philbin was an Internal Revenue Service agent in 1957 when Jim Roederer asked him to be an honorary coach for the All-College Tournament.

John Philbin was inducted into the All-College Hall of Fame in 2004. Twenty years earlier he appeared at a reception following his wedding to Peggy Tourchot. *Courtesy Oklahoma Publishing Company.*

University of Oklahoma basketball standout Wayman Tisdale. *Courtesy Oklahoma Publishing Company.*

When Philbin showed up at the airport to greet the Temple University coach, he offered to pick up his luggage. Not accustomed to such Midwestern hospitality, the coach thought Philbin was trying to steal the luggage.

The stint as honorary coach struck a chord with Philbin. He enjoyed mingling with the coaches and players at the All-College Tournament and accompanying events.

As a longtime president of the ASA, he spent thousands of hours preparing for the All-College, although not all moments were glorious. Once after a coach lost a game, he chewed out Philbin for what he perceived to be lousy officiating. The chewing out was on television, prompting many of Philbin's friends to say, "You deserved it! If you're going to be president, you have to deal with the problems, too!"

Philbin was inducted into the All-College Hall of Fame in 2004. His 41 years of service on the ASA board, along with Jack Moncrief, is the longest in the organization's history. He was ASA treasurer for 22 years and president for nine years. He is a senior shareholder in the law firm of Speck Philbin. When asked why the ASA and the All-College have been so successful, Philbin said, "Oklahoma hospitality is what set us apart."

BILLY TUBBS

Billy Tubbs grew up in Tulsa and always was aware of the existence of the All-College tournament. However, he first appeared in the classic in 1972 as an assistant coach at North Texas State University.

Tubbs graduated from Lamar University and was men's basketball coach at that university from 1976 to 1980 when he became coach at OU. After 15 seasons leading the Sooners' men's basketball team, he coached at Texas Christian University from 1994 to 2002.

Tubbs was known for his run-and-gun high-scoring offense. He took the Sooners to the NCAA championship game in 1988. He won 11 All-College crowns—eight in a row. He won five conference titles, 13 post-season appearances, and six consecutive "Sweet Sixteen" appearances. He was Big Eight coach of the year four times and was national coach of the year in 1983 and 1985. Overall, Tubbs compiled a 641-340 record in 31 coaching seasons. He is one of a handful of coaches to win 100 games at three different schools. He had 18 20-win seasons. As one of the host teams of the All-College in the 1980s, Tubbs most remembers 1988 when the tournament featured his team, OSU and Coach Eddie Sutton, Texas and

Coach Tom Penders, and Texas A & M and Coach Shelby Metcalfe. OU beat A & M 128-80 and Texas 124-95 to win the championship.

Tubbs was one of the driving forces to begin the coaches' golf tournament as part of the All-College Tournament festivities. The event drew some of the nation's finest coaches.

Tubbs believes leadership in the All Sports Association is what made sports promotions in Oklahoma City among the most successful in the country. Tubbs was inducted into the All-College Hall of Fame in 2006.

Former University of Oklahoma Coach Billy Tubbs gives a moment of instruction to Sooner star Brent Price. *Courtesy University of Oklahoma Athletic Department.*

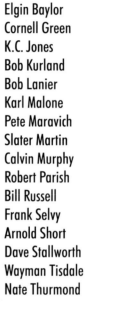

Elgin Baylor	Seattle
Cornell Green	Utah State
K.C. Jones	San Francisco
Bob Kurland	Oklahoma State
Bob Lanier	St. Bonaventure
Karl Malone	Louisiana Tech
Pete Maravich	Louisiana State
Slater Martin	Texas
Calvin Murphy	Niagara
Robert Parish	Centenary
Bill Russell	San Francisco
Frank Selvy	Furman
Arnold Short	OCU
Dave Stallworth	Wichita State
Wayman Tisdale	Oklahoma
Nate Thurmond	Bowling Green

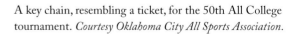

A key chain, resembling a ticket, for the 50th All College tournament. *Courtesy Oklahoma City All Sports Association.*

ALL-COLLEGE CHAMPIONS

YEAR	CHAMPION	RUNNER-UP	SCORE	YEAR	CHAMPION	RUNNER-UP	SCORE
1936	Oklahoma A&M	University of Tulsa	40-17	1962	Loyola (Chicago)#	Wyoming	93-82
1937	Oklahoma A&M	Southwestern, Kansas	26-22	1963	Wichita State University	Oklahoma City University	80-47
1938	Warrensburg, Missouri State	University of Texas	33-25	1964	DePaul University	Oklahoma City University	67-60
1939	Oklahoma A&M	Texas Tech University	37-34	1965	Oklahoma City University	Virginia Tech	99-90
1940	Pittsburg, Kansas State	University of Texas	39-38	1966	Montana State University	Oklahoma City University	82-81
1941	West Texas State	Oklahoma A&M	37-31	1967	Oklahoma City University	Brigham Young University	91-88
1942	Texas Christian University	University of Arkansas	37-25	1968	Louisiana State University	Duquesne	94-91
1943	University of Oklahoma	Norman Navy	31-27	1969	Niagara	Oklahoma City University	87-75
1944	Oklahoma A&M#	University of Arkansas	43-29	1970	Utah State	Louisiana State University	97-81
1945	Oklahoma A&M#	Baylor	65-46	1971	Eastern Kentucky	Oklahoma City University	83-78
1946	Oklahoma A&M	University of Kansas	43-39	1972	Long Beach State	Brigham Young University	101-89
1947	Oklahoma A&M	University of Texas	32-31	1973	Southern California	Oral Roberts University	76-75
1948	Oklahoma A&M	Baylor	39-26	1974	Centenary College	Oklahoma City University	91-80
1949	Oklahoma City University	Wyoming	36-35*	1975	Long Island University	Centenary College	80-78
1950	Oklahoma A&M	Arkansas University	54-41	1976	Virginia Military Institute	Oklahoma City University	69-58
1951	Oklahoma City University	University of Tulsa	52-41	1977	San Francisco	Arizona State	102-90
1952	Oklahoma A&M	Idaho	51-49	1978	New Mexico State	Weber State	63-58
1953	Oklahoma A&M	Santa Clara	67-56	1979	University of Oklahoma	Louisiana Tech	80-70
1954	San Francisco#	George Washington University	73-57	1980	Oklahoma State University	University of Idaho	94-83
1955	University of Tulsa	Oklahoma City University	65-58	1981	Lamar	Rhode Island	63-51
1956	Seattle	Oklahoma City University	70-69*	1982	Oklahoma State University	Oklahoma City University	76-64
1957	San Francisco	Oklahoma City University	60-45	1983	University of Oklahoma	Arkansas/Little Rock	87-62
1958	Oklahoma City University	Duquesne	75-59	1984	University of Oklahoma	Louisiana Tech	84-72
1959	Utah State	Oklahoma City University	75-59	1985	University of Oklahoma	Southern Methodist University	92-69
1960	Wichita State University	Baylor	76-74	1986	Texas Christian University	University of Oklahoma	95-82
1961	Bowling Green	Houston	47-45	1987	University of Oklahoma	Illinois State University	107-56

YEAR	CHAMPION	RUNNER-UP	SCORE
1988	University of Oklahoma	University of Texas	124-95
1989	University of Oklahoma	University of Tulsa	99-78
1990	University of Oklahoma	University of Tulsa	112-99
1991	University of Oklahoma	Texas Christian University	78-73
1992	University of Oklahoma	University of Texas	85-76
1993	University of Oklahoma	University of Tulsa	95-76
1994	University of Oklahoma	University of Tulsa	76-61
1995	University of Florida	University of Oklahoma	76-72*
1996	University of Tulsa	University of Oklahoma	78-75
1997	University of Oklahoma	University of Alabama	79-61
1998	University of Oklahoma	Oral Roberts University	85-69
1999	University of Oklahoma	Arkansas State University	64-51
2000	University of Oklahoma	Southern Methodist University	79-78*
2001	University of Oklahoma	Texas Southern University	97-55
2001	Oklahoma State University	Ball State University	82-70
2003	University of Oklahoma	Michigan State University	60-58
	Oklahoma State University	Brigham Young University	78-65
2004 (Jan.)	University of Oklahoma	Princeton	58-55
	Oklahoma State University	Southern Methodist University	89-54
2004 (Dec.)	University of Oklahoma	University of Tulsa	70-64
	Gonzaga	Oklahoma State University	78-75
2005	Oklahoma State University	University of Tennessee	89-73
	University of West Virginia	University of Oklahoma	92-68
2006	University of Oklahoma	University of Tulsa	58-48
	Oklahoma State University	University of Pittsburg	90-87

#Won NCAA Championships Same Season   *Overtime

University of Oklahoma	22
Oklahoma State University	18
Oklahoma City University	5
University of San Francisco	3
Wichita State University	2
Utah State University	2
Texas Christian University	2
University of Tulsa	2
Loyola University (Chicago)	1
University of Florida	1
Niagara University	1
DePaul University	1
Seattle University	1
West Texas State University	1
Pittsburg, Kansas State	1
Warrensburg, Missouri State	1
New Mexico State University	1
Louisiana State University	1
Montana StateUniversity	1
Eastern Kentucky University	1
Long Beach State University	1
Southern California University	1
Centenary College	1
Long Island University	1
Virginia Military Institute	1

1936

Robert Jones	Tulsa
Dick Krueger	Oklahoma A&M
Hubert Kirkpatrick	Baylor
Merle Rousey	Oklahoma A&M
Carl Brown	Tulsa

1937

Lloyd Tucker	SW Kansas
Eddie Hinshow	SW Kansas
Ray Hamilton	Arkansas
Dick Krueger	Oklahoma A&M
Harvey Slade	Oklahoma A&M

1938

Al Shirk	Warrensburg, MO
Frank Bryski	Baylor
James Biggs	Warrensburg, MO
Bobby Moers	Texas
Harvey Slade	Oklahoma A&M

1939

Johnny Adams	Arkansas
Marshall Brown	Texas Tech
Jesse Renick	Oklahoma A&M
Howard Doyle	Oklahoma A&M
Harvey Slade	Oklahoma A&M

1940

LeRoy Ohlehap	Pittsburg, KS
Lonnie Eggleston	Oklahoma A&M
W .B. Houpt	Texas
Don Sturdy	Pittsburg, KS
Udell Moore	Texas

1941

Price Brookfield	West Texas
Lonnie Eggleston	Oklahoma A&M
Charles Halbert	West Texas
Frank Stockman	West Texas
Dwight Parks	Baylor

1942

Bill Blackmon	Texas Christian
Bill Closs	Rice
Gordon Carpenter	Arkansas
Bob McHenry	Texas Christian
Clayton Wynne	Arkansas

1943

Ken Pryor	Oklahoma
Rem Meyer	Norman Navy
Bob Kurland	Oklahoma A&M
Jesse Renick	Norman Navy
Allie Paine	Oklahoma

1944

Weldon Kern	Oklahoma A&M
Harold Hines	Oklahoma
Bob Kurland	Oklahoma A&M
Bill Flynt	Arkansas
Bill Henry (tie)	Rice
Glark Johnson (tie)	West Texas

1945

Paul Courry	Oklahoma
Weldon Kern	Oklahoma A&M
Charlie Black	Kansas
Bob Kurland	Oklahoma A&M
Jackie Robinson	Baylor

1946

John Hargis	Texas
Joe Bradley	Oklahoma A&M
Charlie Black	Kansas
A. L. Bennett	Oklahoma A&M
Ray Evans	Kansas

1947

A. L. Bennett	Oklahoma A&M
Slater Martin	Texas
Bob Harris	Oklahoma A&M
Herb Gergman	Georgia Tech
Jackie Robinson	Baylor

1948

Don Heathington	Baylor
J. L. Parks	Oklahoma A&M
Bob Harris	Oklahoma A&M
Slater Martin	Texas
Bill Johnson	Baylor

1949

Loy Doty	Wyoming
A. E. Lemons	Oklahoma City
Jack Shelton	Oklahoma City
Farrel Craig	Oklahoma City
John Pitch	Wyoming

1950

Don Johnson	Oklahoma A&M
Bob Schneider	Alabama
Bob Ambler	Arkansas
Gale McArthur	Oklahoma A&M
D. L. Miller	Arkansas

1951

Dick Haag	Wyoming
Andy Likens	Oklahoma City
Don Penwell	Oklahoma City
Don Johnson	Oklahoma A&M
Dick Nunneley	Tulsa

1952

Gerald Stockton	Oklahoma A&M
Dwight Morrison	Idaho
Bob Mattick	Oklahoma A&M
Hartley Kruger	Idaho
Arnold Short	Oklahoma City

1953

Harry Jorgensen	Wyoming
Kenneth Sears	Santa Clara
Bob Mattick	Oklahoma A&M
Frank Selvy	Furman
Arnold Short	Oklahoma City

1954

Bill Russell	San Francisco
Bob Patterson	Tulsa
Cleo Littleton	Wichita
Jerry Mullen	San Francisco
Walter Devlin	George Washington

1955

Junior Born	Tulsa
Joe Sturgis	Penn
Mack Carter	Oklahoma A&M
Les Roh	Idaho State
V. R. Barnhouse	Oklahoma A&M

1956

Elgin Baylor	Seattle
Hubert Reed	Oklahoma City
Win Wilfong	Memphis State
Dick Sticklin	Seattle
Jim McCoy	Marquette

1957

Alex "Boo" Ellis	Niagara
Mike Farmer	San Francisco
Hubert Reed	Oklahoma City
Gene Brown	San Francisco
Fred LaCour	San Francisco

1958

Bob Slobodnik	Duquesne
Roger Wendel	Tulsa
Fred Moses	Oklahoma City
Bub Sahmaunt	Oklahoma City
Jimmy Darrow	Bowling Green

1959

Jimmy Darrow	Bowling Green
Max Perry	Utah State
Al Butler	Niagara
Cornell Green	Utah State
Jerry Schofield	Utah State

1960

Cornell Green	Utah State
Ron Heller	Wichita
Fred Moses	Oklahoma City
Lanny VanEman	Wichita
Gene Wiley	Wichita

1961

Nate Thurmond	Bowling Green
Ernie Moore	Wichita
Howard Komives	Bowling Green
Cornell Green	Utah State
Gene Wiley	Wichita

1962

Jerry Harkness	Loyola (Chicago)
George Kirk	Memphis
Glynn Robinson	Wyoming
Paul Silas	Creighton
Les Hunter	Loyola (Chicago)

1963

Dave Stallworth	Wichita
Bud Koper	Oklahoma City
Bennie Lennox	Texas A&M
Glynn Robinson	Wyoming
Don Schverak	Houston
Ernie Moore	Wichita

1964

Steve Thomas	Xavier
Jesse Nash	DePaul
Jim Murphy	DePaul
Jerry Lee Wells	Oklahoma City
Elton McGriff	Creighton

1965

Steve Chubin	Rhode Island
Jerry Lee Wells	Oklahoma City
James Ware	Oklahoma City
John Wetzel	Virginia Tech
Ted Ware	Virginia Tech

1966

Gary Gray	Oklahoma City
Bill Tindall	Massachusetts
Tom Storm	Montana State
Jack Gillespie	Montana State
Art Harris	Stanford

1967

Rich Travis	Oklahoma City
Kari Liimo	Brigham Young
Glen Combs	Virginia Tech
Bob Quick	Xavier
Wally Tinker	Auburn

1968

Pete Maravich	Louisiana State
Carl Asheley	Wyoming
Johnny Arthurs	Tulsa
Garry Nelson	Duquesne
Bob Lanier	St. Bonaventure

1969

Calvin Murphy	Niagara
Wayne Jones	Niagara
Willie Watson	Oklahoma City
Bobby Croft	Tennessee
Jimmy England	Tennessee

1970

Jeff Tebbs	Utah State
Nate Williams	Utah State
Al Sanders	Louisiana State
Bill Brickhouse	Montana State
John Nelson	Oklahoma City

1971

Charlie Mitchell	East Kentucky
Mike Stewart	Santa Clara
Marvin Rich	Oklahoma City
George Bryant	East Kentucky
Greg Lowery	Texas Tech

1972

Ed Ratleff	Long Beach
Ozzie Edwards	Oklahoma City
Reggie Royals	Florida State
Belmont Anderson	Brigham Young
Doug Richards	Brigham Young

1973

Phil Sellers	Rutgers
Louis Dunbar	Houston
Sam McCants	Oral Roberts
Sidney Edwards	Houston
Dan Anderson	Southern California

1974

George Jackson	UNCC
Earl King	NTSU
Robert Parish	Centenary
Jon Manning	Oklahoma City
Leon Johnson	Centenary

1975

Robert Parish	Centenary
Barry McLeod	Centenary
Ed Gregg	Utah State
Nate Bland	Centenary
Ernie Douse	Long Island

1976

Ron Carter	VMI
Will Bynum	VMI
Gregg Krause	Oklahoma City
Clydell Tucker	Oklahoma City
Arthur Edwards	Baylor

1977

Winford Boynes	San Francisco
Lamont Reid	Oral Roberts
Archie Aldridge	Miami (Ohio)
Blake Taylor	Arizona State
Ernie Cobb	Boston College

1978

Albert Jones	New Mexico State
Bruce Collins	Weber State
Londale Theus	Santa Clara
Greg Webb	New Mexico State
Mike Edwards	New Orleans

1979

Joe Ivory	Louisiana Tech
Kenny Cunningham	West Michigan
Rubin Jackson	Oklahoma City
Terry Stotts	Oklahoma
Ken Lyons	North Texas State

1980

Matt Clark	Oklahoma State
Ken Lyons	North Texas State
Albert Irving	Alcorn State
Leroy Combs	Oklahoma State
Ken Owens	Idaho

1981

Rubin Jackson	Oklahoma City
Joe Dystra	Western Illinois
Terry Long	Lamar
Marc Upshaw	Rhode Island
Chuckie Barnett	Oklahoma

1982

Matt Clark	Oklahoma State
Leroy Combs	Oklahoma State
Lorenca Andrews	Oklahoma State
James Campbell	Oklahoma City
Don Williams	UT Arlington

1983

Wayman Tisdale	Oklahoma
Tim McCalister	Oklahoma
Donald Newman	Arkansas-Little Rock
George Clayton	Oklahoma City
Mike Rivers	Arkansas-Little Rock

1984

Wayman Tisdale	Oklahoma
Darryl Kennedy	Oklahoma
Karl Malone	Louisiana Tech
Anthony Bowie	Oklahoma
Tim Cain	Manhattan

1985

Tim McCalister	Oklahoma
Darryl Kennedy	Oklahoma
Anthony Bowie	Oklahoma
Kevin Lewis	Southern Methodist
Muhammad Akar	Oklahoma State

1986

Jamie Dixon	Texas Christian
Carven Holcombe	Texas Christian
Darryl Kennedy	Oklahoma
Harvey Grant	Oklahoma
Gary Swain	Creighton

1987

Harvey Grant	Oklahoma
Mookie Blaylock	Oklahoma
B.J. Armstrong	Iowa
Roy Marble	Iowa
Haywoode Workman	Oral Roberts

1988

Mookie Blaylock	Oklahoma
Mike Bell	Oklahoma
Tyrone Jones	Oklahoma
Byron Houston	Oklahoma State
Royce Jeffries	Oklahoma State
Joey Wright	Texas

1989

Tony Martin	Oklahoma
Skeeter Henry	Oklahoma
Terry Evans	Oklahoma
Marcell Gordon	Tulsa
Barry Mayberry	Arkansas State

1990

Andy Kennedy	Alabama-Birmingham
Marcell Gordon	Tulsa
Kermit Holmes	Oklahoma
Reggie Shields	Tulsa
Brent Price	Oklahoma

1991

Damon Patterson	Oklahoma
Michael Strickland	Texas Christian
Brent Price	Oklahoma
Brett Roberts	Morehead State
Reggie Smith	Texas Christian

1992

Albert Burditt	Texas
Bryan Sallier	Oklahoma
Bryatt Vann	Oklahoma
Terrence Rencher	Texas
Stan Rose	Weber State

1993

Jeff Webster	Oklahoma
Shea Seals	Tulsa
Ryan Minor	Oklahoma
Dion Barnes	Oklahoma
Mark Davis	Texas Tech

1994

Ryan Minor	Oklahoma
Shea Seals	Tulsa
Alvin Williamson	Tulsa
Kurt Thomas	Texas Christian
Kirk Fortenberry	Alabama State

1995

Ryan Minor	Oklahoma
Doug Brandt	Baylor
Tyrone Fisher	Oklahoma
Dametri Hill	Florida
LeRon Williams	Florida

1996

Shea Seals	Tulsa
Rod Thompson	Tulsa
Janthony Joseph	Western Illinois
Nate Erdmann	Oklahoma
Corey Brewer	Oklahoma

1997

Shea Seals	Tulsa
Rod Thompson	Tulsa
Janthony Joseph	Western Illinois
Nate Erdmann	Oklahoma
Corey Brewer	Oklahoma

1998

Corey Brewer	Oklahoma
Evan Wiley	Oklahoma
Antoine Brockington	Coppin State
Mike Dillard	Sam Houston State
Brian Williams	Alabama

1999

Chris Bjorklund	Cal Poly
Joe Harney	Western Kentucky
Chad Wilkerson	Oral Roberts
Ryan Humphrey	Oklahoma
Eduardo Najera	Oklahoma

2000

Jerryl Sasser	Southern Methodist
Willie Davis	Southern Methodist
Damon Hancock	Southern Methodist
Kelly Newton	Oklahoma
Mire Chatman	UTPA
Nolan Johnson	Oklahoma

2001

Theron Smith	Ball State
Victor Williams	Oklahoma State
Ebi Ere	Oklahoma
Jason Detrick	Oklahoma
Maurice Baker	Oklahoma State

2002

Ebi Ere	Oklahoma
Hollis Price	Oklahoma
Chris Hill	Michigan State
Travis Hansen	Brigham Young
Ivan McFarlin	Oklahoma State

2003

Jamie Rosser	Arkansas State
Chico Fletcher	Arkansas State
Lubos Barton	Valparasio
J.R. Raymond	Oklahoma
Eduardo Najera	Oklahoma

2004 (January)

Daniel Bobick	Oklahoma State
Tony Allen	Oklahoma State
DeAngelo Alexander	Oklahoma
Ed Persia	Princeton
Bryan Hopkins	Southern Methodist

2004 (December)

Jaison Williams	Oklahoma
Steven Graham	Oklahoma State
John Lucas	Oklahoma State
Adam Morrison	Gonzaga
J. P. Batista	Gonzaga

2005

Chris Lofton	Tennessee
Kevin Pittsnagle	West Virginia
Taj Gray	Oklahoma
JamesOn Curry	Oklahoma State
David Monds	Oklahoma State

2006

Rod Earls	Tulsa
Austin Johnson	Oklahoma
Mario Boggan	Oklahoma State
JamesOn Curry	Oklahoma State
Aaron Gray	Pittsburg

INDIVIDUAL RECORDS

POINTS - 61
WAYMAN TISDALE,
Oklahoma vs. Texas/San Antonio, 1983

FIELD GOALS - 24
WAYMAN TISDALE,
Oklahoma vs. Texas/San Antonio, 1983

FREE THROWS - 19
LYNDON LEE,
Oklahoma City vs. Tulsa, 1963

REBOUNDS - 22
WAYMAN TISDALE,
Oklahoma vs. Texas/San Antonio, 1983

3 POINT FIELD GOALS - 8
TERRY EVANS,
Oklahoma vs. North Texas, 1989

3 POINT FIELD GOAL ATTEMPTS - 17
TERRY EVANS,
Oklahoma vs. North Texas, 1989

ASSISTS - 14
RICKEY GRACE,
Oklahoma vs. Texas, 1988

STEALS - 8
MOOKIE BLAYLOCK,
Oklahoma vs. Texas, 1988;
vs. Illinois State; and vs. Oral
Roberts, 1987

BLOCKED SHOTS - 10
BRIAN SKINNER,
Baylor vs. Louisiana Tech, 1995

TEAM RECORDS

POINTS - 147
Oklahoma vs. North Texas,
(147-94), 1989

FIELD GOALS - 56
Oklahoma vs. Oral Roberts, 1987

FREE THROWS - 39
Arizona State vs. Boston
College, 1977

REBOUNDS - 71
Oklahoma vs. Oral Roberts, 1987

3 POINT FIELD GOALS - 17
Oklahoma vs. North Texas, 1989

3 POINT FIELD GOAL ATTEMPTS - 37
Oklahoma vs. North Texas, 1989

ASSISTS - 32
Oklahoma vs. North Texas, 1989

STEALS - 18
Oklahoma vs. North Texas, 1989

PERSONAL FOULS - 38
Tulsa vs. Oklahoma, 1990

FEWEST POINTS - 16
Baylor vs. Oklahoma A & M, 1944

FEWEST FIELD GOALS - 5
Baylor vs. Oklahoma A & M, 1944

FEWEST FREE THROWS - 1
Florida State vs. Brigham Young, 1972

FEWEST PERSONAL FOULS - 6
Oklahoma vs. St. Bonaventure, 1968

TWO TEAMS (TOTAL)

POINTS-241
Oklahoma (147) vs. North Texas (94), 1989

FIELD GOALS - 95
Oral Roberts (52) vs. Houston (43) 1973

FIELD GOAL ATTEMPTS - 203
Oklahoma (115), vs. North Texas (88), 1989

PERSONAL FOULS - 68
Oklahoma A & M (33) vs. Idaho (35), 1951

REBOUNDS - 130
Oklahoma (64) vs. North Texas (66), 1989

3 POINT FIELD GOALS - 23
Oklahoma (17) vs. North Texas (6), 1989

3 POINT FIELD GOAL ATTEMPTS - 53
Oklahoma (37) vs. North Texas (16) 1989

FEWEST POINTS - 43
Oklahoma A & M (22) vs. Baylor (21), 1947

FEWEST FREE THROWS - 7
Texas Tech (4) vs. Texas Christian (3), 1943

FEWEST FIELD GOALS - 11
Oklahoma A & M (6) vs. Baylor (5), 1947

FEWEST PERSONAL FOULS - 17
Texas Christian (9) vs. Norman Navy (8) 1943

LARGEST MARGIN OF VICTORY - 53
Oklahoma (147) vs. North Texas (94) 1989

INDIVIDUAL RECORDS

MOST POINTS - 84
WAYMAN TISDALE
Oklahoma, 1983

FIELD GOALS - 33
WAYMAN TISDALE
Oklahoma, 1983

REBOUNDS - 32
HARVEY GRANT
Oklahoma, 1987

3 POINT FIELD GOALS - 10
TERRY EVANS
Oklahoma, 1989

3 POINT FIELD GOALS
ATTEMPTS - 24
TIM MCCALLISTER
Oklahoma, 1986

ASSISTS - 23
RICKY GRACE
Oklahoma, 1987

STEALS - 16
MOOKIE BLAYLOCK
Oklahoma, 1987

TEAM RECORDS

POINTS - 252
Oklahoma, 1988

HIGHEST SCORING AVERAGE - 126
Oklahoma, 1988

FIELD GOALS - 97
Oklahoma, 1987

FIELD GOAL ATTEMPTS - 199
Oklahoma, 1987

FREE THROWS MADE - 61
Oklahoma, 1984

FREE THROW ATTEMPTS - 80
Oklahoma, 1989

REBOUNDS - 112
Oklahoma, 1987

3 POINT FIELD GOALS - 20
Oklahoma, 1989

3 POINT FIELD GOAL ATTEMPTS - 48
Oklahoma, 1987

ASSISTS - 56
Oklahoma, 1987

STEALS - 31
Oklahoma, 1987, 1989 & 1991

THREE GAMES TEAM RECORDS

POINTS - 303
Oklahoma City, 1965

HIGHEST SCORING AVERAGE - 101
Oklahoma City, 1965

FIELD GOALS - 129
Oklahoma City, 1965
Oral Roberts, 1973

FREE THROWS MADE - 90
Georgia Tech, 1956

PERSONAL FOULS - 91
Auburn, 1948
Idaho, 1951

FEWEST POINTS - 86
Baylor, 1947

FEWEST FIELD GOALS MADE - 24
Baylor, 1947

FEWEST FREE THROWS MADE - 11
Texas Christian, 1943

HIGHEST SCORING AVERAGE - 101
Oklahoma City, 1965

FIELD GOALS - 129
Oklahoma City, 1965
Oral Roberts, 1973

FREE THROWS MADE - 90
Georgia Tech, 1956

PERSONAL FOULS - 91
Auburn, 1948
Idaho, 1951

FEWEST POINTS - 86
Baylor, 1947

FEWEST FIELD GOALS MADE - 24
Baylor, 1947

FEWEST FREE THROWS MADE - 11
Texas Christian, 1943

ALL-COLLEGE CLASSIC INDIVIDUAL AWARDS

YEAR	MOST VALUABLE PLAYER	LEADING SCORER	GAMES	POINTS
1951	Don Penwell, Oklahoma City	Dick Nunneley, Tulsa	3	46
1952	Arnold Short, Oklahoma City	Arnold Short, Oklahoma City	3	70
1953	Bob Mattick, Oklahoma A&M	Frank Selvy, Furman	3	121
1954	Bill Russell, San Francisco	Bob Patterson, Tulsa & Cleo Littleton, Wichita	3	70
1955	Junior Born, Tulsa	Les Roh, Idaho State	3	80
1956	Elgin Baylor, Seattle	Elgin Baylor, Seattle	3	76
1957	Alex "Boo" Ellis, Niagara	Alex Ellis, Niagara	3	84
1958	Bud Sahmaunt, Oklahoma City	Roger Wendel, Tulsa	3	70
1959	Max Perry, Utah State	Jimmy Darrow, Bowling Green & Al Butler, Niagara	3	76
1960	Lanny Van Eman, Wichita State	Cornell Green, Utah State	3	74
1961	Nate Thurmond, Bowling Green	Cornell Green, Utah State & Darnel Haney, Utah State	3	69
1962	Flynn Robinson, Wyoming	Flynn Robinson, Wyoming & Ray Wolford, Toledo	3	76
1963	Dave Stallworth, Wichita State	Dave Stallworth, Wichita State	3	92
1964	Jim Murphy, DePaul	Steve Thomas, Xavier	3	101
1965	James Ware, Oklahoma City	Steve Chubin, Rhode Island	3	95
1966	Tom Storm, Montana State	Bill Tindall, Montana State	3	98
1967	Rich Travis, Oklahoma City	Rich Travis, Oklahoma City	3	113
1968	Pete Maravich, Louisiana State	Pete Maravich, Louisiana State	3	138*
1969	Calvin Murphy, Niagara	Calvin Murphy, Niagara	3	75
1970	Jeff Tebbs, Utah State	Al Sanders, Louisiana State	3	72
1971	Charlie Mitchell, E. Kentucky	Greg Lowery, Texas Tech	3	87
1972	Ed Ratleff, Long Beach State	Ed Ratleff, Long Beach State	3	87
1973	Phil Sellers, Rutgers	Phil Sellers, Rutgers	3	101
1974	George Jackson, UNCC	George Jackson, UNCC & Earl King, North Texas State	3	76
1975	Robert Parish, Centenary	Robert Parish, Centenary	3	70
1976	Ron Carter, VMI	Ron Carter, VMI	3	68
1977	Winford Boynes, San Francisco	Lamont Reid, Oral Roberts	3	84
1978	Albert Jones, New Mexico State	Londale Theus, Santa Clara	3	77
1979	Kenny Cunningham, Western Mich	Kenny Cunningham, Western Mich	3	83

YEAR	MOST VALUABLE PLAYER	LEADING SCORER	GAMES	POINTS
1980	Matt Clark, Oklahoma State	Matt Clark, Oklahoma State	3	77
1981	Terry Long, Lamar University	Reuben Jackson, Oklahoma City	3	78
1982	Matt Clark, Oklahoma State	Matt Clark, Oklahoma State	2	37
1983	Wayman Tisdale, Oklahoma	Wayman Tisdale, Oklahoma	2	**84
1984	Darryl Kennedy, Oklahoma	Darryl Kennedy, Oklahoma	2	51
1985	Tim McCalister, Oklahoma	Tim McCalister, Oklahoma & Kevin Lewis, Southern Methodist	2	48
1986	Jamie Eixon, Texas Christian	Gary Swain, Creighton	2	50
1987	Harvey Grant, Oklahoma	Harvey Grant, Oklahoma	2	70
1988	Mookie Blaylock, Oklahoma	Mookie Blaylock, Oklahoma	2	52
1989	Tony Martin, Oklahoma	Tony Martin, Oklahoma	2	57
1990	Kermit Holmes, Oklahoma	Andy Kennedy, Alabama/Birmingham	2	60
1991	Damon Patterson, Oklahoma	Brett Roberts, Morehead State	2	62
1992	Bryan Sallier, Oklahoma	Stan Rose, Weber State	2	54
1993	Jeff Webster, Oklahoma	Jeff Webster, Oklahoma	2	56
1994	Ryan Minor, Oklahoma	Kurt Thomas, Texas Christian	2	67
1995	Ryan Minor, Oklahoma	Ryan Minor, Oklahoma	2	52
1996	Shea Seals, Tulsa	Shea Seals, Tulsa	2	52
1997	Corey Brewer, Oklahoma	Antoine Brockington, Coppin State	2	49
1998	Eduardo Najera, Oklahoma	Chris Bjorklund, Cal Poly	2	50
1999	Eduardo Najera, Oklahoma	Eduardo Najera, Oklahoma	2	45
2000	Nolan Johnson, Oklahoma	Jerryl Sasser, Southern Methodist	2	38
2001	Maurice Baker, Oklahoma State	Maurice Baker, Oklahoma State	1	22
2003	Ebi Ere, Oklahoma	Ivan McFarlin, Oklahoma State	1	27
2004 (Jan.)	DeAngelo Alexander, Oklahoma	DeAngelo Alexander, Oklahoma	1	22
	Daniel Bobik, Oklahoma State	Daniel Bobik, Oklahoma State & Tony Allen, Oklahoma State & Joey Graham, Oklahoma State	1	14
2004 (Dec.)	J.P. Baptista, Gonzaga	Stephen Graham, Oklahoma State	1	22
	Jaison Williams, Oklahoma	Jaison Williams, Oklahoma	1	21
2005	Taj Gray, Oklahoma	Taj Gray, Oklahoma	1	31
	David Monds, Oklahoma State	Chris Lofton, Tennessee	1	21
2006	Mario Boggan, Oklahoma State	Mario Boggan, Oklahoma State	1	30
	Rod Earls, Tulsa	Rod Earls, Tulsa	1	16

YEARS PRIOR TO 1951 NOT AVAILABLE

EXPANDING HORIZONS

Although the All Sports Association was founded to save the annual All-College Tournament in Oklahoma City, it was not long until organization leaders realized the benefits of hosting a variety of sporting events. Numbers crunched by government officials did not lie—a huge economic shot-in-the-arm could result from supporting events that would appeal to the diverse fan base in the metropolitan area. Not only was there an economic benefit, an expanded variety of sports gave bragging rights for attracting new businesses to locate in the area.

In the first few months after ASA was founded, executive secretary Stanley Draper, Jr., convinced coaches of the four major college basketball schools in Oklahoma to play a doubleheader. The event was dubbed the "Big 4 Doubleheader," and was played on December 17, 1957, at Municipal Auditorium in Oklahoma City. OU played Tulsa and OCU played OSU.

In February, 1958, the ASA sponsored games in the National Industrial Basketball League between the Phillips 66ers, the Amateur Athletic Union team sponsored by Phillips Petroleum Company, and teams from Peoria, Illinois, and Wichita, Kansas.

In April, 1958, Draper and the ASA Board of Directors hosted a post-season tour of National Basketball Association star players. The top 20 players in the league appeared in a game on the all-star tour. Also in 1958, the ASA took over sponsorship of the Celebrities Softball Game. The 1958 contest featured celebrities from the Oklahoma City area on two teams—the Featherheaded Greenies and the Mudville Sluggers. There was also a Fourth of July holiday amateur baseball tournament that year.

Wanting to expand to high school sports, ASA board members conceived the idea to host an 11-team area high school football preview on September 11, 1958. Eight thousand fans jammed Taft Stadium to see players from Capitol Hill, Southeast, Northeast, Douglass, and Central high schools compete against youngsters from Catholic, Harding, Classen, U.S. Grant, and John Marshall high schools. Each school received $926.45 from the proceeds.

The annual high school prep preview continued until 1970 and raised more than $150,000 for area high schools in the 12-year period.

The fall of 1959 brought two professional sports to Oklahoma. In September, ASA hosted an NFL exhibition game between the Detroit Lions and the Philadelphia Eagles at Owen Field. In October, the St. Louis Hawks played the Cincinnati Royals in an NBA exhibition contest at Municipal Auditorium.

The following year, from June 9-12, ASA joined with Twin Hills Golf and Country Club to host the Oklahoma City Open Golf Tournament that featured top-ranking professionals including Arnold Palmer, winner of the Masters and the U.S. Open.

As the variety of events sparked interest in all kinds of sports in Oklahoma City, the ASA put together a highly successful baseball train to take fans to Kansas City for a weekend series between the Kansas City Athletics and the Baltimore Orioles. Baseball interest was at an all-time high because of the possibility of Oklahoma City becoming the top farm team for the new Houston Colt .45's major league team. ASA President Jim Roederer was one of the principal spokesmen for the group of Oklahoma City leaders who ultimately convinced Houston to select Oklahoma City for the honor. Oklahoma City had been absent from the world of professional baseball for four years.

One of the most unique All Sports Association promotions was to bring the Russian national champion hockey team to Oklahoma City. In this photograph, John Philbin announces the 1994 visit of the hockey team. Part of the package also was an appearance of the Russian Ballet Troupe, although that performance never happened in Oklahoma City. *Courtesy Oklahoma City All Sports Association.*

Part of the attraction for a Triple-A minor league franchise for Oklahoma City was the city council's approval of construction of a 10,000-seat stadium at the state fairgrounds. The park was called All Sports Stadium, a tribute to the contributions that the ASA made in solidifying interest among fans and corporate leaders to bring minor league baseball back to Oklahoma City. Roederer became the first president of the Oklahoma City 89ers.

The All Sports Association played such an integral role in pushing for construction of a stadium at the State Fairgrounds in Oklahoma City, the city council named the facility "All Sports Stadium." The stadium opened in 1962. Courtesy Oklahoma City All Sports Association.

The ASA continued to host professional exhibition games and, in December, 1961, presented the first annual All Sports Bowl, featuring junior college teams from Langston University and Panhandle A & M in Goodwell, Oklahoma.

The ASA, fresh from its victory in helping win a minor league baseball franchise, went to work advocating a multi-purpose assembly center to be built in downtown Oklahoma City. Jim Roederer announced in June, 1962, that more than 30,000 signatures were needed on a petition to show city leaders that sports fans and business leaders would relish the idea of building a huge convention center that could host both sporting and commercial events.

The ASA campaign and the work of many other citizens and groups resulted in the construction of the Myriad Convention Center, completed in 1972 as one of the finest convention centers in the United States. A 15,000-seat arena was surrounded by two dozen meeting rooms, a Great Hall for large banquets, and 100,000 square feet of exhibition space for conventions and trade shows. The Myriad covered four blocks in downtown Oklahoma City and had nearly one-million square feet of space under one roof.

While the Myriad was in planning and construction stages, the ASA was busy expanding its horizons. In 1962, the group assisted the Oklahoma City 89ers in its first season ticket sales campaign. In 1964, the ASA arranged a five-year commitment from the Lone Star Conference of Texas and the Oklahoma Collegiate Conference to provide teams for the annual All Sports Bowl. However, the bowl was discontinued after the first year because of lack of fan interest.

Meanwhile, hockey was on the minds of ASA leaders. Jim Roederer attended the winter meeting of the Central Hockey League in 1965. There was talk that Oklahoma City might be able to land a minor league hockey franchise, perhaps a struggling franchise in Minneapolis, Minnesota. Even though the ASA would not financially be involved in such a franchise, it was a great example of the organization's focus on supporting any kind of sport for Oklahoma City.

In January, 1967, Roederer resigned as president of the ASA. In its first decade of existence, Roederer was re-elected annually, but told members in 1967 that his health was declining and he desired to turn over leadership of the group to someone else. His replacement was Thurman Medley.

One of Medley's first actions was to establish the All-College Hall of Fame. Legendary OSU basketball coach Henry P. Iba was selected as the first member of the Hall of Fame. A temporary location for the Hall of Fame was the State Fair Arena.

In September, 1968, softball took center stage as the ASA hosted a World Softball Tournament at All Sports Stadium. Teams from New Zealand, the Philippines, Canada, Mexico, Japan, the Bahamas, Puerto Rico, Venezuela, South Africa, the Virgin Islands, and the United States participated in the event.

In 1976, the All Sports Association hosted the 73rd American Bowling Congress Tournament at the Myriad Convention Center. Lee Allan Smith was chairman of the event that boasted the largest purse in bowling history. In this photograph, ASA President Carl Grant introduces that year's All-Sports queen and her court during bowling tournament festivities. *Courtesy Oklahoma City All Sports Association.*

**ALL SPORTS
NATIONAL COLLEGE
BASKETBALL COACHES**

**GOLF
INVITATIONAL
1st ANNUAL**

JULY 6-8, 1988

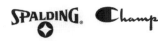

The program for the All Sports Association's Golf Invitational in 1988. *Courtesy Oklahoma City All Sports Association.*

**PARTICIPATING COACHES
NATIONAL BASKETBALL COACHES GOLF INVITATIONAL
JULY 6-8, 1988**

Gene Bartow *University of Alabama - Birmingham*	**Shelby Metcalf** *Texas A & M University*
Dave Bliss *University of New Mexico*	**Mike Newell** *University of Arkansas*
Jim Boeheim *Syracuse University*	**Tom Penders** *University of Texas*
Tom Davis *University of Iowa*	**Dean Smith** *University of North Carolina*
Hugh Durham *University of Georgia*	**Bob Staak** *Wake Forest University*
Leonard Hamilton *Oklahoma State University*	**Norman Stewart** *University of Missouri*
Don Haskins *University of Texas - El Paso*	**Eddie Sutton** *University of Kentucky*
Moe Iba *Texas Christian University*	**Jerry Tarkanian** *University of Nevada - Las Vegas*
Gene Iba *Baylor University*	**Ken Trickey** *Oral Roberts University*
Gene Keady *Purdue University*	**Billy Tubbs** *University of Oklahoma*
Jim Killingsworth *Texas Christian University*	**Glenn Wilkes** *Stetson University*
Bob Knight *Indiana University*	**Gary Williams** *Ohio State University*
Abe Lemons *Oklahoma City University*	**Tom Young** *Old Dominion University*

An impressive list of nationally-known basketball coaches attended the 1988 Golf Invitational. All Sports Association volunteers spent hundreds of hours in making the tournament a success. *Courtesy Oklahoma City All Sports Association.*

After the Myriad Convention Center opened in November, 1972, the ASA hosted one of the facility's first events. OU, OSU, OCU, and Tulsa University played in a Big Four Doubleheader on December 1.

In 1973, ASA played host to the general assembly of the International Sports Federation at the Myriad. It was the first time the meeting was held outside Europe.

In 1985, an All-College, All-Time tournament team was announced. Fifteen players, one coach, one sportscaster, and one sports information director were included. The team included Coach Henry Iba, sportscaster Curt Gowdy, Sports Information Director Pete Rozelle of San Francisco University, and players Elgin Baylor, Cornell Green, K.C. Jones, Bob Kurland, Bob Lanier, Pete Maravich, Slater Martin, Calvin Murphy, Robert Parish, Bill Russell, Frank Selvy, Arnold Short, Dave Stallworth, Nate Thurmond, and Wayman Tisdale. The team was honored at a banquet at the National Cowboy Hall of Fame.

The December, 1985 tournament drew 20,479 fans, a record since the tournament had been reduced from eight to four teams in 1982.

It took a lot of letter writing to resolve a possible conflict with the NCAA at the 1987 All-College basketball tournament. ASA officials decided to give 12-speed bicycles to the student athletes who would take part in the All-College. After the bicycles were shipped to the universities in early December, the NCAA notified the ASA that such gifts were in violation of rules of awarding non-personalized items such as trophies and letter-jackets to collegiate players.

ASA President Glenn Boyer wrote the NCAA, "We are extremely disappointed and shocked to find our gifts this year are not one that can be condoned by your office. We paid less than $70 each for the bicycles, which is less than half the cost of watches previously given to the players in past All-College tournaments."

The NCAA denied an exemption to the rules. Richard Evrard, director of NCAA Legislative Services, wrote each of the four schools and informed the players that acceptance of the bicycles could result in disciplinary action. The crisis was averted when the ASA suggested that each player donate his bicycle to a local charity in their university city. That program worked, and dozens of needy children had an ASA-purchased bicycle for Christmas.

More than 75,000 candles lit
Oklahoma Memorial Stadium
in Norman during the opening
ceremonies of the 1989 U.S.
Olympic Festival. *Courtesy Oklahoma
Publishing Company.*

Olympic Festival athletes show
their enthusiasm during the
opening ceremonies of the 1989
spectacular. *Courtesy Oklahoma
Publishing Company.*

A NEW BEGINNING

In 1988, after 31 years of collaboration with the Oklahoma City
Chamber of Commerce, the ASA decided to set up its own offices and hire
its own staff. Until that time, the ASA used the chamber's office space and
staff. ASA President Glenn Boyer told reporters there was no rift with the
chamber but it was time for the organization to "strike out on its own."

Part of chamber employee Wilma Goodin's responsibility was to
assist Stanley Draper, Jr., in All Sports activities. When ASA decided to set
up its own office, Draper asked Goodin to become a full-time ASA staff
member. It was exciting working for Draper. Goodin, who remains with ASA
more than 30 years after she joined the chamber staff, said, "Back before
computers, Stanley would decide on a Friday afternoon to do a mailing to
300 to 400 people. We brought in volunteers, typed letters, and stuffed
envelopes until dark."

Also in 1988, coaches Abe Lemons and Billy Tubbs hosted the All
Sports National Basketball Coaches Golf Tournament at Oak Tree Golf and
Country Club. The event was successful and attracted many of the nation's
top basketball coaches.

Diversity in ASA events was becoming prevalent in 1988 with the adoption
of the BMX Grand Nationals bicycle event. The November holiday event was
the first booked at the Myriad by the Oklahoma City Chamber of Commerce
to help fill the void following the loss of the National Finals Rodeo in 1984.
After an initial three-year run, the event was taken to new levels by the ASA for
ten years, with thousands of competitors and families coming to Oklahoma City.
The competition had to find a new home after 1997 due to renovation of the
Myriad exhibit hall.

In 1989, the ASA was a prime sponsor of the National Sports Festival, a huge undertaking that included competition in 38 events. It was billed as the Olympic Festival and was part of the centennial celebration of the Land Run of 1889 that opened central Oklahoma to settlement.

In 1989, the ASA assumed sponsorship of Aerospace America, an annual air show that had been initiated three years earlier by the Oklahoma City Chamber of Commerce. When the chamber announced its intention to drop sponsorship of the event, ASA took over and continued the event for nearly another decade. Huge losses due to inclement weather during some of the events caused the ASA board to withdraw its sponsorship of the air show.

Working the Aerospace America events provided board member Joe Groves with some of his fondest memories. "We were a top air show in the world," Groves said, "Just a few of the many headliners were the United States Air Force Thunderbirds, the Navy Blue Angels, and Canadian Forces Snowbirds." Groves especially remembers the first public appearance of the SR-71 Blackbird.

In 1990, ASA added rodeo to the mix by courting the International Professional Rodeo Association. The group's International Finals Rodeo was held at the Myriad, bringing many visitors to Oklahoma City and drawing large local crowds.

LEFT: Don Douglas, a 24-year board member, served as president of the ASA from 1998 to 2000. Accomplishments during his presidency included the hiring of executive director Tim Brassfield, implementation of a successful business plan, debt retirement, and cultivation of sponsor and conference relationships. His tenure also saw a broader community base with new board members. *Courtesy Oklahoma City All Sports Association.*

RIGHT: ASA president John Philbin and Coach P. J. Carlisimo at the ASA annual golf invitational. *Courtesy Oklahoma City All Sports Association.*

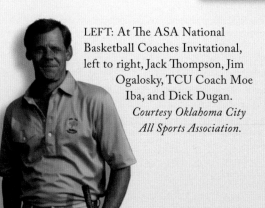

LEFT: At The ASA National Basketball Coaches Invitational, left to right, Jack Thompson, Jim Ogalosky, TCU Coach Moe Iba, and Dick Dugan. *Courtesy Oklahoma City All Sports Association.*

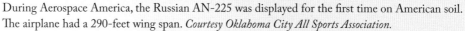

During Aerospace America, the Russian AN-225 was displayed for the first time on American soil. The airplane had a 290-feet wing span. *Courtesy Oklahoma City All Sports Association.*

The ASA often helped staff and support other sporting events. For example, in 1990, ASA staff and volunteers helped present *The Daily Oklahoman* Track Classic at the Myriad and the Virginia Slims tennis tournament at the Greens Golf and Country Club.

In 1992 the ASA continued to host the International Finals Rodeo, the BMX Grand Nationals, the Sooner Indoor Invitational track meet, the National Basketball Coaches Golf Invitational, and the NCAA wrestling tournament.

In 1999, Stanley Draper, Jr. decided to retire after 42 years as executive secretary or executive director of the ASA. He spent May 31, his last day on the job, in the press box at the Women's College World Series, which he brought to Oklahoma City. World Series Director Marita Hynes said, "Stanley was the one who had the vision to know what the tournament could be and when no one else was ready to take a chance on it, he stayed with it."

Huge crowds gathered at Will Rogers World Airport for Aerospace America. In 1991 it was estimated 145,000 people attended the event. *Courtesy Oklahoma City All Sports Association.*

Oklahoma-born
American astronaut
Thomas P. Stafford,
second from left,
visits with a Russian
cosmonaut and
representatives of the
Russian space program
at Aerospace America.
*Courtesy Oklahoma City
All Sports Association.*

As with most All Sports Association sponsored events, Aerospace America required a huge cast of volunteers. At a party for more than 200 volunteers and sponsors of the air show in 1989 were, left to right, Leroy Hansen, H. C. McClure, Glenn Boyer, Edye Draper, and Stanley Draper, Jr. *Courtesy Oklahoma Publishing Company.*

A series of newspaper stories lauded Draper's efforts, including his major role in saving NCAA indoor track. Draper was replaced by Tim Brassfield, who literally hit the ground running to carry on events that were in progress. Brassfield, a former OU gymnast with 20 years experience in the athletic products industry, made marketing a new focus of the ASA. Brassfield said, "I felt we needed to establish our brand, to make sure people understood everything that the ASA did." Brassfield found that outside of a few dozen corporate sponsors, few people knew the extent of ASA's contributions to the community.

The leadership of ASA that set the group apart from other civic and charitable endeavors is "in good hands" with Brassfield. Lee Allan Smith said, "He is a workhorse just like Stanley Draper, Jr. Tim is a great public relations expert and tends to every detail to make All Sports Association as successful as possible."

Brassfield continues to guide his staff with precision. An action plan is developed and implemented for each major event. Months before an event, dozens of committees of volunteers begin their work. Staff members work with board members to coordinate the gargantuan efforts of hundreds of volunteers.

"ASA is perhaps the best vehicle to advertise our city and state," Brassfield proclaims. "Now, through major national events such as the NCAA Women's College World Series and conference and regional competition, Oklahoma City is showcased in hundreds of hours of national television programming each year. That is the kind of advertising you can't buy!"

Brassfield's goal is to make certain ASA continues as a stronghold in collegiate championships, to remain in the rotation for hosting major events, and expand ASA's amateur youth base. His dream is to someday have a facility adjacent to the Oklahoma River such as Disney's Wide World of Sports in Florida.

In 2004, ASA sponsored the McDonald's High School All-American games at the Ford Center. In 2005, the NCAA Division I men's Midwest basketball regional was held in Oklahoma City and staff and members worked much of the year on planning for a large number of collegiate championships on the horizon.

The variety of sporting events hosted by ASA in 2006-2007 included the NCAA Women's College Softball World Series, the Big 12 Conference baseball tournament, the OG&E Sooner State Summer Games, the OKC All Sports Golf Invitational, the Double Sport Apparel/ESPNU Wrestling Invitational, the NCAA Wrestling Championship, the Big 12 softball championship, and the Big 12 men's and women's basketball championships.

Leaders of the community always stand ready to assist the All Sports Association in its projects. Lee Allan Smith, left, talks with Allen Coles in 1984 about promotion for the All-College. Smith, who has observed the first 50 years of ASA's work in Oklahoma City, said, "The economic impact of All Sports Association projects is phenomenal. Great leadership has kept the organization going for a half century when other worthy projects fell by the wayside." *Courtesy Oklahoma Publishing Company.*

Golf tournaments always bring together sponsors, volunteers, and celebrities. Left to right, longtime Oklahoma State University basketball coach Eddie Sutton and board members John Philbin and Bill Nashert. *Courtesy Oklahoma City All Sports Association.*

LEFT: ASA staff and interns at the 2001 All Sports Association Golf Tournament. *Courtesy Lonnie Brewer and Brent Webb.*

To commemorate the signing of a contract to host the International Finals Rodeo are officials of the All Sports Association and the International Rodeo Association (IRA). ASA's hosting of the rodeo was a major factor in the IRA's decision to move its headquarters to Oklahoma City. *Courtesy Oklahoma City All Sports Association.*

HIGHLIGHTS OF
ALL SPORTS ASSOCIATION EVENTS

• ASA has co-sponsored 30 NCAA Division I championships;

• The NCAA Women's College Softball World Series continues to be one of the collegiate sports' fastest growing championships;

• ASA is the only host agency to be associated with NCAA basketball since its inception in 1939;

• The O'Reilly All-College Basketball Classic is the world's oldest basketball tournament;

• The annual Phillips 66 Big 12 Conference Baseball Championship is the largest baseball tournament in the world except for the College World Series;

• The annual Sooner State Games is Oklahoma's only amateur sports festival, featuring competition at venues across the state. Thousands of athletes participate in a variety of events from basketball to ice skating.

BEHIND THE SCENES OF A CHAMPIONSHIP

By Dick Dugan

While the All Sports Association has been securing and hosting events for 50 years, a look at its biggest event ever provides some insight to the diverse activities required for success. The presentation of the 2007 Big 12 Men's and Women's Basketball Championships represent the culmination of experience and organization gained by the ASA over the years, and reveals just what these men and women do.

Before you host an event, you first have to land it. The ASA has established a solid foundation for championships and has earned the confidence of the Big 12 conference. But the dynamics and magnitude of this attractive event require exceptional synergy. There will be strong bids from major market competitors, Dallas and Kansas City. An enthusiastic host committee consisting of five organizations pulling together with the ASA is formed to develop the bid, and later execute the event.

Extensive efforts produced a most attractive bid to submit in April, 2005. It featured key benefits such as central location and adequate hotel rooms, with the scheduled opening of the renovated Skirvin Hotel exemplifying the renaissance of the community. The biggest factor of exclusivity and merit is across-the-street proximity of the men and women venues. Considering that enhancement of the women's championship is a conference priority, the bid includes major up-grades to the Cox Convention Center arena and a guarantee of ticket revenue far exceeding the requirement. To solidify the proposal, additional incentives such as airline trips and lodging accommodations for event preparation visits to Oklahoma City are offered.

The Oklahoma City Mayor's office plays a key role in leadership with strong commitments from the city. Mayor Mick Cornett makes many appearances from contacts with conference officials to addressing pep rallies and attending games.

The Office of City Manager places a high priority on the event requirements. Responsibilities include the Ford Center and $2.5 million in improvements at the Cox Convention Center. Street closing, security and event parking are also part of executive manager Tom Anderson's high-level assignment for the event.

The Greater Oklahoma City Chamber of Commerce takes the lead for communications that include media relations and promotional advertising. A DVD player in a hi-tech look case, along with a custom CD that features Oklahoma City is given to conference officials and school VIPs just prior to the bid submittal. The positioning statement of "58 Steps between Championships" proves to be very successful, both in the bid submittal and for promotion throughout the event. "Our objective is to be creative and positively differentiate our city," said Cynthia Reid, Chamber Vice President-Marketing & Communications. "The coaches and school administrators will remember the custom logo dart boards that they received shortly after the bid was awarded. And their attention was tweaked each of the six times they received two darts, each with a conference school name, every so often before the event."

The chamber also assists with securing complimentary lodging for the contractual package. They also have responsibility for hospitality functions, which are very important for conference relations.

The Oklahoma City Convention and Visitors Bureau makes a special effort to coordinate with the hotels for host information, decorations, and event signage. Communication with the Bricktown merchants is a priority as well.

Downtown Oklahoma City, Inc. takes on special efforts for downtown and airport signage, plus maps and directional signage to parking. Their recruitment and provision of uniformed OKC Ambassadors to serve as information providers on the street during the event is a huge asset for extending hospitality to the visiting fans.

And, of course, there is the All Sports Association, a well-organized group of experienced staff, board members, and cadre of energetic interns. ASA works closely with the conference staff in a multitude of assignments. ASA's operational responsibility is up close and in detail. Execution must be precise and in accord with the 27-section, 100 page-plus operational manuals for both the Men's and Women's championships. The staff and two board member co-chairs is the kingpin of coordination with all of the other entities, including volunteers.

Committees are established that pretty much mirror the structure that ASA has sharply honed for its collegiate events over the years. However, for this major Big 12 event there is some variation from the norm in chairing and staffing the committees.

Matt Bown, co-chair of the men's Team Host Committee, recruits and guides community conscious volunteers for this important function. "Each team host is usually a board member," said Bown. "But because there are actually two tournaments with the men and women, and the field of each is 12 teams, our 42 board members are all co-chairing various committees." But the volunteers, such as bank executive Jim Daniel, are well qualified and naturals. He was the team host for Baylor University, his alma mater.

The team host serves as a concierge for the team to make sure that their stay in Oklahoma City is great. We want them to want to come back to our great city. Introduction and a welcome are extended during contact with their director of operations prior to team arrival. Hosts greet their team on arrival, coordinate getting the coaches their courtesy car keys, attend all practices and assist with any reservations or requests. They have even been known to assist with late night laundry.

Although each team is responsible for their own air and bus travel arrangements, the Transportation Committee has many responsibilities. Co-chair Sam Ott says, "Much of the work is done in advance—collecting information from all of the coaches, conference officials, and administrators so that they will not have to deal with forms and formalities upon arrival. Financial arrangements are made with rental car companies and pick-up and delivery of vehicles to the hotels is coordinated. The first days of arrival are really busy." Ott said, "We just strive to make everything convenient, like with little things such as placing welcome greeting notes in their cars, each customized with their team logo and containing contact information." Other responsibilities include volunteers to man the transportation headquarters, which provides VIP shuttle service to the airport throughout the event.

Transportation for and coordination with game officials is handled by the Officials Committee. Some of the details normally handled by ASA board members are coordinated by conference staff for this conference championship.

"The visiting fan experience is a huge element in all ASA events," says Sandy Price, board member and chairperson of the Alumni Relations Committee. "We provide the groups information well in advance for hotels, transportation, parking, restaurants, and party spaces. We also assist with on-site meeting and booth space, as well as coordinate their pep rallies." Other important functions are coordination with the host hotels for signage and decorations. Restaurants need to be apprised of peak business periods for proper staffing. Responsibilities include providing material and volunteers for information desks in the hotel lobbies.

The fan experience is augmented by the work of the FanFest Committee. They play an important role in the overall atmosphere of the venue. The FanFest area is a popular gathering place between games and features displays, game activities, refreshments, and even live radio and television broadcasts.

Glen Morgan has co-chaired the Hospitality Committee for many years. "We always provide a place for our working board members to relax and enjoy some comradery, as well as entertain sponsors," says Morgan. The Big 12 requires more functions, such as board members filling shifts to serve as hosts for the conference administrator hospitality room.

A walk-through at the venues, both the Ford and Cox centers, the week before the championships provides a final review of other committee's responsibilities. These committees, consisting of co-chairs and volunteers, have met many times regarding their duties which primarily have to do with the games themselves. It requires an insatiable love for basketball and community service for the long hours that are required to accommodate 12 sessions and 22 games in five days.

The Operations Committee's work begins well in advance of the event. Off-site practice sites are arranged. Scheduling is done by the team host, many times at the last minute. Inside the arena the committee administers the dressing rooms, training room, and medical room. The committee is also responsible for the ball boys and ball girls.

The Greeting & Security Committee workers are stationed at the designated check-in area for the teams. They serve as greeters and escort the teams to their locker rooms, as well as assist with stringent control of issuing credential pins to a specific 22-person roster. Additional duties include assisting trainers in getting their equipment to the locker rooms.

Working in the same general area of the entrance is the Band & Cheerleader Committee. They check in a maximum of 29 members for each band, plus the director, 12 spirit squad members, and one mascot. Equipment is checked by security and cheerleaders are escorted to a warm-up area. The committee worker escorts the band to their designated area, and sits with the band to monitor compliance with conference guidelines. Board member Bill Leeper has traditionally headed up this committee. Leeper said, "The work is fun. Sometimes your ears hurt a little after sitting so close to the bands. And even though the students are well briefed on rules, they are sometimes difficult to control. We got a little reprimand when Texas was doing a low-key drum roll during opponent free throws."

Experience—Organization—Teamwork—Time—Dedication. The results are:

- 200,000 fans and visitors and 24 teams, providing an economic impact of $40 million for Oklahoma City,
- 63 hours of television exposure,
- a sellout in only four months for the men's championship, a first time overtime championship game,
- 113,274 total attendance,
- a record-breaking 27% increase in overall attendance of 48,990 for the women's championship,
- outstanding accolades from fans, school administrators, and conference officials, and a huge dose of pride for our robust community.

The final proof of the success of the event was realized when it was announced three months later that Oklahoma City would again host the championship event in 2009!

University of Kansas basketball star
Kirk Hinrich won the Abe Lemons
Award in 2001. *Courtesy Oklahoma
Publishing Company.*

THE ABE LEMONS AWARD

The Abe Lemons Award was established in 2000 to honor the nation's leading three-point shooter from the previous year. The first winner was Jason Thornton of the University of Central Florida. In 2007, the award criterion was changed to honor the top offensive player in NCAA Division I men's basketball. ASA partnered with the Parkinson Foundation of the Heartland to present the Abe Lemons Memorial Hoopla, an annual fund raising event that serves as the venue to present the award. In his final years, Lemons was stricken with Parkinson's Disease.

Ben Byers, ASA board member and Abe Lemons Award program chairman, said, "It is a privilege for ASA to honor Abe with this award. He was a great friend of our association."

Lemons won the hearts of basketball fans on the court and in real life. He coached at Oklahoma City University, the University of Texas, and Pan American University. He won 599 games and produced many All-Americans during his coaching years from 1955 to 1990. His light-hearted look at life and his true concern for his players and others made him loved by almost everyone—including referees he had sparred with over the years. He was a national coach of the year in college basketball and is a member of the Oklahoma Sports Hall of Fame and the Oklahoma Hall of Fame.

Abe Lemons was a highly successful basketball coach, not only for his winning teams on the court, but for shaping the lives of young men who became stellar citizens of the community. *Courtesy Oklahoma Publishing Company.*

ABE LEMONS AWARD WINNERS

2000 – Jason Thornton	University of Central Florida
2001 – Kirk Hinrich	University of Kansas
2002 – Dante Swanson	University of Tulsa
2003 – Brad Lechtenerg	San Diego University
2004 – Salim Stoudamire	University of Arizona
2005 –Stephen Sir	University of Northern Arizona
2006—Kevin Durant	University of Texas

A saddle bronc rider scores points in the International Finals Rodeo at the Myriad Convention Center. The ASA presented the IFR competition from 1990 to 1995. *Courtesy International Professional Rodeo Association.*

SCHOLARSHIP PROGRAM

Consistently focusing on the future is a priority of the All Sports Association—and that includes attention to youth and the development of leaders and future stakeholders in the community. Not only has an aggressive intern program been developed in recent years, but a new scholarship program rewards outstanding girls and boys and encourages them to give back to their community.

Two $1,000 scholarships are awarded to an outstanding boy and girl each year. Recipients of scholarships are selected on criteria consistent with the mission of the ASA. Student achievement in leadership, character, athletics, and academics are considered.

RECIPIENTS

2004
Shanna Sprinkle   Deer Creek High School
Zachary Taylor   Del City High School

2005
JoDee Schmidt   Coyle High School
Brad Boydston   Westmoore High School

2006
Denesh Roseburr   Northeast Academy
Joel Ziebell   Casady High School

2007
Rachel Ratcliffe   Norman North High School
Matthew Deimund   Putman City North High School

The scholarships are funded by a special fund that has been established at the Oklahoma City Community Foundation. *Courtesy Oklahoma City All Sports Association.*

The 2006 NCAA Wrestling Championship was the first chanpionshhip held at Oklahoma City's new Ford Center. *Courtesy Oklahoma City All Sports Association.*

HOSTING CHAMPIONSHIPS

One of the first championships landed by the All Sports Association was a sports oddity. In 1974, the ASA hosted the United States Table Tennis Association's tournament which brought teams from 16 countries to Oklahoma City. It was the largest championship in that sport for the entire year.

In 1977, ASA hosted its first sub-regional of the NCAA Men's Basketball Championship. Marquette University was the Oklahoma City regional winner and went on to win the national championship that year. While the regionals are not true championship games, they are a huge part of March Madness and Final Four frenzy. This regional event, as well as NCAA Midwest Regionals in 1994, 1998, 2003, and 2005 provided invaluable national exposure for Oklahoma.

In the early 1980s, the ASA began a concentrated effort to bring collegiate championships to Oklahoma City. In March, 1981, the ASA and the Oklahoma City Chamber of Commerce successfully won a bid to host the NCAA wrestling tournament for 1983. It was the first time the event was held off a university campus.

The ASA paid for an advertising campaign to attract fans to the tournament. Local media also did an outstanding job in promoting the competition that drew fans to matches even when Oklahoma schools were not involved.

The 1983 NCAA wrestling tournament at the Myriad was a huge success. With Glenn Boyer as ASA president, the tournament had advance ticket sales of $447,000, a record for the national tournament. More than 9,000 all-session tickets were sold—also a record.

Collegiate events continued to be a highlight of ASA promotions. The NCAA wrestling tournament continued to draw huge crowds to the Myriad. In 1985, the NCAA Division I women's tennis tournament was held at the Myriad. Paid attendance was double any previous national women's tennis tournament sponsored by the NCAA.

Bryce Drew hit the game-winning shot against Mississippi in Valparaiso's first round upset in the 1998 NCAA Men's Tournament. With only 2.5 seconds remaining, two passes covered 94 feet to get the ball to Drew who made a 23-foot jumper to cinch the upset. *Sports Illustrated* ranked the shot the # 5 sports moment of 1998. *Courtesy Oklahoma City All Sports Association.*

The Big Eight Conference baseball championship was held in Oklahoma City since its inception in 1976 until the conference changed to the Big 12 in 1997. After the Big 12 Conference was formed, the baseball championship was hosted by the All Sports Association every year from 1997 to 2007 except for two. The event was held in Arlington, Texas, in 2002 and 2004. The ASA has now reached an agreement for Oklahoma City to be the home of the Big Twelve baseball championship.

In 1987, the ASA began hosting the NCAA men's and women's indoor track and field championships at the Myriad Convention Center. The following year, the event drew nearly 5,000 fans, a record. Television money began to be a major source of income for the ASA. The ASA was paid $38,000 for the broadcast rights to the All-College by local and state networks following their teams.

The University of Kansas won the Big Eight women's tennis championship in Oklahoma City in 1995. The All Sports Association hosted the tournament the same week in which a bomb destroyed the Alfred P. Murrah Federal Building in downtown Oklahoma City. *Courtesy Oklahoma City All Sports Association.*

The Ford Center was the site of an ESPN University wrestling invitational featuring the University of Oklahoma, Oklahoma State University, Hofstra University, and the University of Minnesota in 2006. *Courtesy Oklahoma City All Sports Association.*

RIGHT: The top six competitors in the 1,000-meter run at the NCAA Track & Field Championship in Oklahoma City in 1987. *Courtesy Oklahoma City All Sports Association.*

LEFT: Oklahoma City's Myriad Convention Center was home to the NCAA Indoor Track & Field Championships in 1986 and 1987. The All Sports Association was the host of the event. *Courtesy Oklahoma City All Sports Association.*

Night games were especially popular for fans at the Big Eight baseball championship at All Sports Stadium. *Courtesy Oklahoma City All Sports Association.*

The ticket brochure for the 1982 Big Eight baseball tournament hosted by the All Sports Association. *Courtesy Oklahoma City All Sports Association.*

In 1999, Tim Allen of the Big Twelve Conference fields questions from reporters during the Big Twelve baseball tournament. *Courtesy Oklahoma City All Sports Association.*

Oklahoma State University's Mitch Simmons, left, leaps over Jon Pittenger of the University of Missouri in a 1989 Big Eight baseball championship game. *Courtesy Oklahoma Publishing Company.*

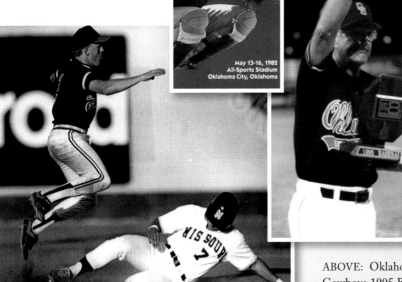

In 1989, the NCAA wrestling tournament returned to the Myriad, and a contract was signed to host the event three years later. In 1990 the ASA hosted both the Big Eight men's and women's tennis championships at the Oklahoma City Tennis Center.

In 1999 the Sooner Athletic Conference men's and women's basketball tournament was hosted by the ASA at the Sawyer Center on the campus of Southern Nazarene University.

ABOVE: Oklahoma State University baseball coach Gary Ward celebrates the Cowboys 1995 Big Eight baseball championship. The Cowboys won the title at All Sports Stadium. *Courtesy Oklahoma Publishing Company.*

The ticket brochure for the 2006 Big Twelve baseball championship played at Oklahoma City's Bricktown Ballpark. *Courtesy Oklahoma City All Sports Association.*

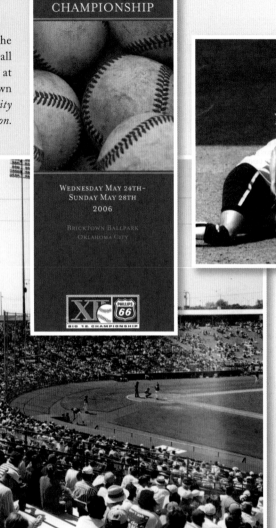

2006 was a busy year for All Sports Association volunteers and staff in hosting several league championships. The Big Twelve women's softball championship was held in mid-May. Two weeks later, the Big Twelve baseball championship came to town, followed by the Women's College World Series the next week. *Courtesy Oklahoma City All Sports Association.*

Hosting conference and national championships in Oklahoma City brings many conference and NCAA officials to town. Tim Allen, the associate commissioner of the Big Twelve Conference, has been to Oklahoma City so many times he feels at home. He said, "Three more trips to Oklahoma City and I will qualify for citizenship and a free set of steak knives!"

Allen began as the media coordinator of the NCAA track and field championships in the 1980s and coordinated publicity surrounding the Big Eight baseball championship. His fondest memories are of old All Sports Stadium where he first arrived while on the athletic department staff at Oklahoma State University. Allen remembered, "For all of its warts, there was something very special about All Sports Stadium. The field was like a goat ranch and the groundskeepers were grossly understaffed. But kids loved playing there. There were special ground rules because of the electric lines in the outfield."

All Sports Stadium is packed to capacity in 1997 for the first Big Twelve baseball championship. The event moved to the Southwestern Bell Bricktown Ballpark in 1998. *Courtesy Oklahoma City All Sports Association.*

RIGHT: In 2005, Oklahoma City's Ford Center was the site of the first and second rounds of the NCAA men's basketball championship. *Courtesy Oklahoma City All Sports Association.*

BELOW: The All Sports Association was a host of the USA Gymnastics Junior Olympic National Championship at the Cox Convention Center in Oklahoma City in 2006. *Courtesy Oklahoma City All Sports Association.*

All Sports Association President Tim Brassfield, left, and Bill Hancock of the NCAA discuss last minute details at the Ford Center prior to the opening game of the Midwest Regional of the NCAA men's basketball championship in 2003. *Courtesy Oklahoma City All Sports Association.*

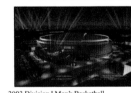

2003 Division I Men's Basketball Midwest Regional
Ticket Application

Hosted by the University of Oklahoma

When the Ford Center was completed in Oklahoma City, the All Sports Association presented the Midwest Regional of the NCAA Men's Basketball Championship in March, 2003. It was the fourth of five NCAA regionals hosted by ASA. Among all regional venues, Oklahoma City is consistently the first to sell out. *Courtesy Oklahoma City All Sports Association.*

One of the greatest quotes from championships at All Sports Stadium was when Iowa State University's Mike Busch hit a long fly ball that hit the leftfield billboard that contained a likeness of the Marlboro Man. Someone in the press box loudly declared, "The game will be delayed for a few minutes while the Marlboro Man leaves to put on a cup!"

BELOW: The Big Twelve Conference baseball championship was held at the AT & T Bricktown Ballpark in Oklahoma City in May, 2007. In 2006, Oklahoma City was named the "home" of the annual conference championship. *Courtesy Oklahoma City All Sports Association.*

Coach Sherri Coale's Oklahoma University Sooners played before a record crowd in winning the 2007 Big Twelve women's basketball championship. *Courtesy Oklahoma City All Sports Association.*

RIGHT: Fans gather outside the Cox Business Services Convention Center in Oklahoma City for the 2007 Big Twelve Conference Women's Basketball Championship. *Courtesy Oklahoma City All Sports Association.*

In March, 2007, the All Sports Association and Oklahoma City hosted both the men's and women's basketball championships of the Big Twelve Conference. It was a monumental feat with the women's championship played at the Cox Convention Center and the men's games played at the nearby Ford Center. Oklahoma City realized an enormously positive economic impact as a result of the event. *Courtesy Oklahoma City All Sports Association.*

Kevin Durant led the University of Texas Longhorns to a 2007 conference championship in the first-ever overtime in a Big Twelve championship final game. *Courtesy Oklahoma City All Sports Association.*

One of the premier sporting events in Oklahoma each year is the NCAA Women's College World Series (WCWS) that brings together the elite eight collegiate teams in women's softball. National television coverage on ESPN gives Oklahoma City incredible publicity. As usual, All Sports Association staff members and a host of volunteers work thousands of hours in preparation for the annual event.

The All Sports Association first hosted the WCWS in 1990, and has brought the event to Oklahoma City every year since with the exception of 1996. That year, the event was held in Columbus, Georgia, as part of the Olympic Games in nearby Atlanta. Attendance has grown from 11,938 in 1990 to a record 62,463 in 2007.

The success of the WCWS is special for board member and event co-chair Shannon Nance. She said, "It has been so exciting to watch the sport grow and thrive in Oklahoma City. We are creating a tradition similar to the men's event in Omaha." The devotion of the fans impresses Nance, "You know the sport and event have staying power when more than 2,000 fans line up at midnight to buy tickets for a rain-delay game and 5,000 fans are still in the stands at 2:00 a.m."

Bringing the College World Series to Oklahoma City did not just "happen." ASA was instrumental in building a strong softball legacy years before. In January, 1965, the ASA successfully competed against five other cities to bring the headquarters of the Amateur Softball Association and the International Softball Association to Oklahoma City. The groups had formerly headquartered in Newark, New Jersey. That move began a continuing love affair between Oklahoma City and softball.

A ticket to the 1991 Big Eight baseball championship tournament in Oklahoma City. *Courtesy Oklahoma City All Sports Association.*

The All Sports Association hosted the first Big Twelve Conference women's softball tournament in 1996. *Courtesy Oklahoma City All Sports Association.*

In 1993, the University of Arizona claimed the NCAA championship at Hall of Fame Stadium in Oklahoma City. *Courtesy Oklahoma Publishing Company.*

1st Annual

Big Twelve Conference Softball Tournament

May 10-11, 1996
ASA Hall of Fame Stadium
Oklahoma City, Oklahoma

It was not an easy battle to land the headquarters of the leading national softball organization and its hall of fame. ASA Vice President Jack Moncrief, Oklahoma softball commissioner W.B. "Bick" Auxier, and Oklahoma City recreation director Alvin R. Eggeling accompanied Stanley Draper, Jr., to a meeting of the softball commissioners in Anaheim, California. By a 70 percent vote, the nation's softball leaders voted to move their headquarters to Oklahoma City. In the fall of 1965, the softball groups moved into temporary offices in Oklahoma City and began planning for construction of a modern stadium and a softball hall of fame. The ASA pledged to secure land for the groups.

The All Sports Association continues a strong partnership with the Amateur Softball Association in growing its world-class faciliity and in execution of the championship games.

BELOW: A ticket to the 2004 Women's College World Series. *Courtesy Oklahoma City All Sports Association.*

ABOVE: Jennie Finch struck out 17 Florida State University batters and hit a home run to advance Arizona to the finals and the 2002 championship. Finch went on to become a gold medalist as a member of the United States Olympic team. *Courtesy Oklahoma Publishing Company.*

LEFT: A professionally produced brochure accompanied tickets for the 2004 Women's College World Series. *Courtesy Oklahoma City All Sports Association.*

ABOVE: Left to right, Don Porter, All Sports President Carl Grant, and an official of the International Softball Federation discuss plans to bring the headquarters of national softball organizations to Oklahoma City. Porter was executive director of the Amateur Softball Association, and its stadium now bears his name. *Courtesy Oklahoma City All Sports Association.*

ABOVE: Coach Patty Gasso rallies her Oklahoma Sooners in the Women's College World Series. *Courtesy Oklahoma City All Sports Association.*

It looks like a softball, but it's a ticket to the 2006 Women's College World Series. *Courtesy Oklahoma City All Sports Association.*

Night games provide a spectacular softball venue at ASA Hall of Fame Stadium. *Courtesy Oklahoma City All Sports Association.*

RIGHT: A colorful pass for the 2005 Women's College World Series. *Courtesy Oklahoma City All Sports Association.*

RIGHT: Kat Osterman of Texas wowed the crowds, as well as the batters, in the Women's College World Series in 2003, 2005, and 2006. *Courtesy Oklahoma City All Sports Association.*

BELOW: Softball fans crowd around women's softball players for autographs after a College World Series game. *Courtesy Oklahoma City All Sports Association.*

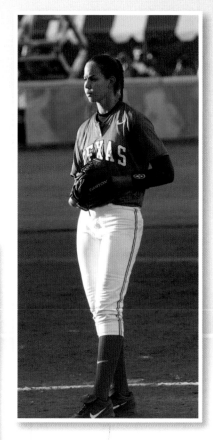

ABOVE: Members of women's collegiate softball teams competing in the College World Series are shown a great time while in Oklahoma City. *Courtesy Oklahoma City All Sports Association.*

RIGHT: Permanent seating capacity at ASA Hall of Fame Stadium was increased from 2,000 to more than 5,000 in 2003. The All Sports Association has been instrumental in the continual enhancement of the stadium, practice fields, and parking areas. *Courtesy Oklahoma City All Sports Association.*

ABOVE: Marketing always has been a strong point in promoting the Women's College World Series. *Courtesy Oklahoma City All Sports Association.*

RIGHT: The nation's top teams compete annually in the Women's College World Series. *Courtesy Oklahoma City All Sports Association.*

ABOVE: UCLA players celebrate after winning the 1992 title as champions of collegiate women's softball. *Courtesy Oklahoma Publishing Company.*

LEFT: Kelly Bongatti of the University of Kansas slides home for a third-inning score as Fresno State University's Christa York bobbles the throw at the plate during a College World Series game in 1992. *Courtesy Oklahoma Publishing Company.*

Kids judo is but one of more than a dozen sports for children in the Sooner State Games. *Courtesy Oklahoma City All Sports Association.*

Several winter sports are available for participants in the Sooner State Games. *Courtesy Oklahoma City All Sports Association.*

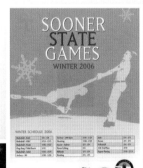

Another ASA innovative program is the Sooner State Games "Lighten Up Oklahoma," a four-month competition that encourages Oklahomans to develop healthy eating habits and active lifestyles. Participants form teams of from two to ten people to compete in two divisions—weight loss and accumulated activity. *Courtesy Oklahoma City All Sports Association.*

LEFT: Archery is one of the sports highlighted in the summer Sooner State Games. *Courtesy Oklahoma City All Sports Association.*

A determined athlete competes in the Sooner State Games. *Courtesy Oklahoma City All Sports Association.*

SOONER STATE GAMES

The Oklahoma Gas and Electric Company (OG&E) Sooner State Games is Oklahoma's Amateur Sports Festival. The first Sooner State Games were held in 1982. The Oklahoma legislature designated the games as the official state games in preparation of the 1989 United States Olympic Festival in Oklahoma City. In 1989, the All Sports Association adopted the program and assumed significant debt.

The annual winter and summer games are based upon the Olympic format and are officially endorsed by the United States Olympic Committee. The games are open to every amateur athlete in the state, regardless of age, sex, or ability. The purpose of the Sooner State Games is to help unite all communities in Oklahoma through sport, health, and wellness. More than 6,000 residents participated in the games in 2007.

THE GOALS OF THE OG&E SOONER STATE GAMES:

1. To help develop Oklahoma's amateur athletic talent into potential Olympians;

2. Bring recognition to gifted Oklahoma athletes and their communities;

3. Provide an opportunity for all Oklahomans to enjoy the benefit of sports played in the spirit of the Olympic creed, which states, "the most significant thing is not winning, but taking part;"

4. Promote the Olympic ideal at the grass-roots community level.

The Sooner State Games provide a five-kilometer, ten-kilometer, and half-marathon run as part of the annual competition. *Courtesy Oklahoma City All Sports Association.*

Winter sports in the Sooner State Games include archery, basketball, billiards, figure skating, karate, ping pong, table tennis, power lifting, racquetball, shooting, speed skating, soccer, tumbling, volleyball, judo, bowling, and trail run.

Events in the summer version of the Sooner State Games include youth basketball, adult basketball, youth baseball, high school baseball, youth softball, adult softball, power lifting, billiards, bowling, ping pong, table tennis, archery, judo karate, shooting, track and field, sand volleyball, 3-on-3 basketball, racquetball, and horseshoes.

Jack Moncrief, the only All Sports Association founding board member still living, is noted for his service in hospitality over the years. He shares many fun and intriguing stories, such as a sidebar to the success story of the Amateur Softball Association (ASA) sales trip to Anaheim, California.

"We were competing strongly with St. Petersburg, Florida, and Lima, Ohio, for the ASA headquarters," said Moncrief. "After an outstanding afternoon presentation, our group learned where the committee hospitality was to be held that evening. We showed up in our All Sports coats, red at that time, and commenced to serve refreshments in our natural hospitable manner. The next day, everyone was commenting how great the OKC All Sports Association social hour was. And someway, the Lima group ended up with the tab."

Moncrief was Director of Physical Education at the YMCA when he served on the ASA organizing committee in 1956. He served as a vice president and chaired hospitality for many years during his 43-year tenure as a board member. He attended more than 12 NCAA Final Fours, recruiting coaches and teams for the All-College, while working the All Sports hospitality suites. *Courtesy Oklahoma City All Sports Association.*

Left to right, board members Sam Ott, Kenny Whittington, Ben Byers and Charles Lutz have fun with a Lebron James stand-up poster promoting the 2004 McDonald's All American Games. Fans saw Candice Parker dunk the basketball in the women's game. Seventeen of the 24 prepsters on the men's teams were playing in the NBA three years later. *Courtesy Oklahoma City All Sports Association.*

WHAT MAKES ASA WORK?

Successful long-term civic projects do not just happen. Behind the memorable first half-century of contributions made by the Oklahoma City All Sports Association are hundreds of board members, volunteers, and staff members who have worked thousands of hours to make ASA-supported projects successful.

Dr. Ken Whittington said, "The board has always been a broad base of professional and blue collar people. A great camaraderie was developed among our group. We got to know each other and enjoyed friendships and the work of the organization."

Board members and volunteers, as honorary coaches, had incredible experiences getting to know teams and coaches. Whittington said, "We pretty much lived with the teams while they were here. We showed them the spirit of Oklahoma." Without volunteers, any ASA project would have fizzled. "We didn't have the money to pay someone to take care of all the minute details," Whittington said, "We did it ourselves!"

Not everything goes as planned at ASA events. Once during the All-College Tournament, the National Anthem performer forgot her words and was in trouble when the lights were dimmed for a moment. She used a cigarette lighter to read her notes, but the paper caught on fire. Whittington remembered, "It was a real mess!"

Longtime board members such as Mark Williams remember special moments with heroes like Abe Lemons. One year Texas Coach Tom Penders saw Lemons in the audience and asked him to give his Longhorn team a pre-game talk. Williams was honored to be in the locker room when Lemons, who had coached at Texas for six years, talked about Texas pride and told the story of how when he was fired at Texas, he wanted a glass-bottomed car so he could see the expression on the athletic director's face as he left town. It was a priceless moment!

Families of board members also get involved in ASA events. Williams' daughters, Cathey and Amy, helped park cars, took tickets, and were inspired by the young athletes they watched. Williams believes the live sporting events always will be an inspiration to fans. He said, "Our events produce visible heroes. When OU won the national softball title in 2000, many of the players had been inspired by watching the same competition a decade before."

Hard work by the professional staff and the board has resulted in increased national attention for sporting events in Oklahoma City. Sportscaster Bob Barry, Jr., who grew up at ASA events under the tutelage of his legendary father, said, "I loved the green jackets the board members wore from the first time I saw them. Even at an early age, I realized that a

ASA office manager Wilma Goodin, right, with former University of Oklahoma basketball coach Billy Tubbs. Wilma is the veteran ASA employee. She is a major asset, working with staff, board members, and countless event ticket customers over the years. Although ASA crowned annual queens in earlier years, there is no doubt Wilma is "Queen of All Sports." *Courtesy Oklahoma City All Sports Association*

Board members such as Jack Thompson were attracted to ASA because of its focus on amateur athletic events that were family-focused. Thompson said, "There was never any personal agenda for anyone on the board. We just tried to do what was best for Oklahoma City."

The enthusiasm of executive director Stanley Draper, Jr., was contagious. Each year when ASA needed to sell event sponsorships and tickets, he walked into the room with a stack of cards and energetically passed them out, giving board members their assignments.

Community leaders depended upon Draper and the ASA. Former Oklahoma City Mayor Ron Norick said, "ASA always had a wonderful reputation as a host. NCAA teams and college groups always gave Oklahoma City rave reviews because of ASA's efforts. Without ASA, the events like we have enjoyed in the past decades would have died. ASA people were the best ambassadors for our city."

huge amount of volunteer work had to be accomplished to produce the All-College tournament and many other events."

Barry said, "ASA has been blessed by two strong directors in its history. Tim Brassfield has followed in the footsteps of Stanley Draper, Jr., as an aggressive leader." About the volunteer effort of the ASA board, Bob Barry, Sr., said, "ASA is made up of pro-Oklahoma people, always positive. No one is lining their pockets. It is a love for Oklahoma that drives them."

Dick Beshear attributes the success of ASA to board members' professional services as well as their commitment of time. He said, "A non-profit organization as large as ours can operate properly only with diverse board members who possess a lot of expertise in various fields, including legal and financial."

ASA officers and board members proudly display the "hardware" to be presented to team and individual champions at the All-College Tournament. *Courtesy Oklahoma City All Sports Association.*

Interns Kim Simpson, left, and Cristen Wolfe sell programs at a Big Twelve Baseball Championship game. The intern program has been a key element in the growth of the All Sports Association. *Courtesy Oklahoma City All Sports Association.*

ASA leaders stick up for each other. In 1989, after newspapers ran a series of stories about exciting sporting events in Oklahoma City such as the air show, the All-College, and BMX races, ASA President John Philbin showed up at the desk of Volney Meece, sports editor of *The Daily Oklahoman.* Displaying a fistful of recent newspaper clippings, Philbin said, "We have 40 people working their tails off. These were good articles, but there was not one word about the All Sports Association." Meece recognized the error and wrote a special column outlining the achievements of the ASA. The column was titled, "All Sports in Search of Identity." Meece gave credit to the 40 ASA board members and the 834 other members who chipped in $60 each to help fund ASA activities.

Former ASA President Arnold Shelley always enjoyed the hectic pace of putting on the All-College Tournament. He said, "We did anything we could to make teams and coaches feel warmly accepted in Oklahoma City. If a volunteer got sick, someone else was waiting in the wings to take his or her job. We just all pitched in together to make the best of every event."

Wilma Goodin, who began working on ASA projects while still employed at the Oklahoma City Chamber of Commerce in 1976, said her more than 30 years of working for the ASA has never been void of excitement. She remembered, "We did rodeos, horse shows, air shows, you name it…and they all worked. I would go to the airport often to pick up some coach or official that I had no idea of what he looked like. I just held up a sign and hoped that he would see it when he got off his airplane."

Glenn Boyer served nearly a decade as ASA president and describes his longtime involvement with the organization as "my sports fix." Boyer, who first appeared in the All-College Tournament as a player, went into the computer business and never followed his sports dream. He said, "The ASA always gave me the greatest opportunity to support sporting events that were great for my family and all the people of Oklahoma City."

Mike Bohrofen, left, and Don Douglas conduct a membership campaign report meeting at the SBC Bricktown Ballpark in 2005. ASA board gatherings are made more interesting by the selection of meeting places that have a sports theme. *Courtesy Oklahoma City All Sports Association.*

The work of the ASA volunteers has drawn great praise. Former OSU baseball coach Gary Ward said, "They always made the clubs the focal point, they never intruded on our time, never asked for credit, and did it year in and year out. ASA put on the best baseball competition in the country."

Former OU baseball coach Enos Semore credits ASA with increasing public interest in collegiate sports. He said, "I saw a great increase in interest in baseball because of the way ASA promoted tournaments. One year we drew 13,000 people, unheard of at the time, better than any other tournament in the country."

In addition to volunteers and paid staff, a lot of the work in producing sporting events now comes from interns, an innovative program between ASA and Oklahoma colleges and universities. Executive Director Tim Brassfield began the program to tap into the talent of students who in turn gain incredible on-the-job training in sporting events production.

Why has ASA been so successful? Some great insight in the quest for an answer to that question comes from Bill Hancock who has decades of experience with the organization. Hancock worked in the OU athletic department, for the Big Eight Conference, and for the NCAA, directing the Men's Basketball Tournament and the Final Four. Hancock works with boards in all major cities wanting to host NCAA events. He said, "Some boards are confused about their identity and their mission—but the All Sports Association never lost the vision of its mission—to bring events to Oklahoma City."

Hancock, who grew up in Hobart, Oklahoma, has seen the transition between ASA's first director, Stanley Draper, Jr., and current director, Tim Brassfield. Hancock said, "A lot of people around the country were concerned about what would happen when Stanley retired. But the transition to Tim worked. He is perfect, unassuming, works hard, takes care of details, stays in the background, and does what he says he will do. He has taken up the baton and is running his race—and Oklahoma is the winner."

Tim Allen, associate commissioner of the Big Twelve Conference, echoes the optimism about the All Sports Association with Brassfield at the helm. Allen said, "Tim has taken the ASA to a new level. Stanley Draper, Jr. and Tim have made the ASA the best organization of its kind in the nation."

Board member James Dickson relaxes after working the scorer's table at the 2004 All-College. *Courtesy Oklahoma City All Sports Association.*

Jack Thompson was president of the All Sports Association from 2001 to 2004. During his term, the ASA moved offices from the Sheraton Century Center to Leadership Square in downtown Oklahoma City. Other milestones achieved included a three-year agreement with ESPN for televising the All-College Classic and the announcement that Oklahoma City would host the 2007 Big 12 Men and Women's Basketball Championship. *Courtesy Oklahoma City All Sports Association.*

Mike Bohrofen was president of the All Sports Association from 2005 to 2007. With the association's growth to a new level, new policies for operation and accountability were implemented. During Bohrofen's administration an employee handbook and a code of ethics were adopted. Also, more business groups and city government became partners with the ASA. *Courtesy Oklahoma City All Sports Association.*

Bill Bumpas became president of the All Sports Association in 2007. He has served on the Board of Directors for 21 years. In recent years, his focus has been the Sooner State Games. *Courtesy Oklahoma City All Sports Association.*

The mission of the All Sports Association could not be accomplished without the involvement and support of individual annual members and business sponsors. Memberships include benefits such as premium seating packages for the All-College Classic, with a portion of the membership fee as net revenue for ASA. In the summer of 2007, the All Sports Association had 820 members—75 percent of them in the higher price "Elite Member" status.

"Loyal members have provided a financial foundation over the years," said president-elect James Dickson, "Their support is critical for our infrastructure and their membership provides a great opportunity for people to be part of a great civic team."

Sponsors, while providing important revenue for the ASA, take advantage of advertising exposure and event ticket packages. Don Douglas said, "We are most appreciative of the business community—both long-time annual sponsors and specific-event sponsors—and funding help from the Oklahoma City Convention and Visitors Bureau."

Walter Gillispie knows the importance of cultivating relationships with sponsors. He said, "Selling sponsorships is a primary responsibility of a board member. And it is not that difficult because we have such a good product and great benefits to offer."

Board member Dale Vaughn especially enjoys his committee work in the area of relationship building. "Our annual golf tournament is a festive event that brings coaches, administrators, civic leaders, sponsors, and members together," Vaughn said, "While it is a fund raiser, the team building benefits are much more important."

Partnerships and common goals make for success. Ed Kelley, editor at *The Oklahoman*, said, "What makes the All Sports Association so special is not just its love of 'all sports,' but its love of Oklahoma City. We at *The Oklahoman* share those passions, and have been honored to work side by side with the ASA in promoting events in the great city we share."

The social and economic impact of the All Sports Association has been evident for a half century. Current ASA President Bill Bumpas said, "Sometimes even we don't recognize the huge impact of the sporting events ASA sponsors. We are so involved in the nuts and bolts of an event we don't see the thousands of fans who eat at local restaurants, stay in area hotels, and infuse large amounts of money into our economy."

"The future is bright," Bumpas proudly proclaims, "With our great board and volunteers, even more events will be attracted to Oklahoma City in the future. We are never satisfied with our past success— we must be even better next year and the next year!"

Keith Price presents the All-College championship trophy to a jubilant University of Oklahoma team. *Courtesy Oklahoma City All Sports Association.*

LEGACIES

All Sports Association board members contribute to and carry on significant traditions of the organization. But there are some cases where there is a legacy of service from generation to generation.

Daniel Medley, who joined the board in 2004, is proud of his ASA heritage. His grandfather, Thurman Medley, was a founding board member and later served as ASA president for 14 years. Daniel's uncle, Dick Medley, served as a board member from 1966 to 1972. Daniel said, "I am proud of the contributions that my grandfather and uncle made and want to serve the association in their honor. The Medley family obviously believes in the worthwhile programs of the association."

Another founding board member, John E. Flood, was followed by his son, John D. Flood.

Gene Cheatham and his son, Tom Cheatham, and Dr. Jim Pitts and his son, Jamie, have served as board members.

Current board member Greg Price was preceded by his board member father, the late Keith Price. Greg tells of one of his best memories involving All Sports relationships, "One day at the old Huckins Hotel during an All Sports meeting, fellow board member Carl Grant convinced my dad to partner with him and purchase the Jacksonville Suns Double-A baseball team. They owned the team for 11 years."

Current father-son board members are Dr. Ken Whittington and his son, Kenny; Don Douglas and son, Scott; and Dick Dugan and son, Drew.

OKC ALL SPORTS ANNUAL SPONSORS

ANNUAL SPONSORS

CORPORATE CHAMPIONS

- AT&T
- ATM Zone
- Gulfport Energy
- Levy Beffort/Grubb & Ellis
- ME/CU
- Midwest Regional Medical Center
- OG&E
- OU Physicians
- The Oklahoman
- Orthopedic Associates

CORPORATE ALL AMERICAN

- Courtyard by Marriott Downtown
- Oklahoma City Marriott
- Renaissance Oklahoma City
  Convention Center Hotel
- Sheraton Oklahoma City Hotel

SOONER STATE GAMES SPONSOR

- Dr Pepper

2007 OFFICERS AND DIRECTORS OF THE ALL SPORTS ASSOCIATION

OFFICERS

Bill Bumpus
President

Mike Bohrofen
Immediate Past President

James Dickson
President Elect

Rob Cherry
Vice President

Kevin Perry
Vice President

Shannon Nance
Vice President

Matt Bown
Vice President

Dick Beshear
Treasurer

Tim Brassfield
Executive Director

BOARD MEMBERS

Kevin Akin
Bob Bergmann
Dick Beshear
Mike Bohrofen
Matt Bown
Tim Brassfield
Bill Bumpus
Ben Byers
Sue Campbell
Rob Cherry
Jeff Cloud
Gary Desjardins
James Dickson
Don Douglas
Scott Douglas
Dick Dugan
Butch Freeman
Walter Gillispie
Steve Griffin
Joe Groves
Jim Hatfield
Bill Leeper
Charles Lutz
Daniel Medley

Tom Miller
Glen Morgan
Shannon Nance
Dr. Barry Northcutt
Sam Ott
Darrel Palmer
Kevin Perry
John Philbin
Greg Price
Sandy Price
D.R. Shipley
Scott Streller
Jack Thompson
Dale Vaughn
Ken Warner
Dr. Ken Whittington
Kenny Whittington
Mark Williams
Dick Champlin*
Drew Dugan*
Mark Kelly*
Dr. Mike Kiehn*
Tony Kyle*
James Monsees*

* Associate

STAFF

Tim Brassfield
Executive Director

Wilma Goodin
Office Manager

Emily Bone
Special Events & Membership Development

Ashlee Nichelson
Public Relations & Event Specialist

Jordan Satarawala
Sponsorships & Marketing

Brad Schmitt
Sooner State Games Manager

Kristi Wilson
Controller

PAST PRESIDENTS & OFFICERS

EXECUTIVE DIRECTORS

Stanley Draper, Jr.
1957-1999

Tim Brassfield
1999-2007

PRESIDENTS

E.L. Jim Roederer
1957-1966

Thurman Medley
1967-1979

Arnold Shelley
1979

Carl Grant
1980-1982

Glenn Boyer
1983-1988

John Philbin
1989-1997

Don Douglas
1998-2000

Jack Thompson
2001-2004

Mike Bohrofen
2005-2006

Bill Bumpus
2007

VICE PRESIDENTS

Thurman Medley
1957-1966

C.H. "Chuck" Simpson
1957-1958

Harold "Scooter" Hines
1958-1960, 1963-1965

Roy Deal
1959-1960

Haskell Mogridge
1961

Gene Cheatham
1962

Jack Moncrief
1964-1965, 1991-1994

Arnold Shelley
1966-1977

Jack Workman
1966-1970

Bill McVey
1971

Ron Norick
1971

Carl Grant
1971-1980

Bob Bunce
1972

Kim Kimberling
1972-1974

Jim Pitts, M.D.
1973-1974

Don McMahon
1975-1977

Dick Champlin
1975, 1981-1987

Jack Hoberecht
1976-1978

Glenn Boyer
1978-1980

Joe Kernke, Jr
1978-1984

Ken Whittington, M.D.
1979-1993

Keith Price
1981-1992

William Nashert, Jr
1985-1997

Jack Thompson
1993-2000

James Dickson
1994-1995, 2001-2004

Pete White
1995

Sam Ott
1995-1997, 2001-2002

Don Douglas
1995-1996

Mike Bohrofen
1996-2000

Greg Price
1997, 2003-2006

Glen Morgan
1998-2000

Ken Warner
1998-2000

Bill Bumpus
1999-2004

Dick Dugan
2001-2006

Rob Cherry
2005-2007

Kevin Perry
2005-2007

Shannon Nance
2007

Matt Bown
2007

TREASURERS

Theron Elder
1957

Harold "Scooter" Hines
1958-1960

Roy Deal
1959-1961

Leon Penn
1962-1964

Harold "Scooter" Hines
1965

John Philbin
1966-1989

James Thielke
1990-1993

Layton Perry
1994-1996

Ken Warner
1997

Sam Ott
1998-2000

Butch Freeman
2001-2004

James Dickson
2005-2006

Dick Beshear
2007

PAST BOARD MEMBERS

NAME	YEARS SERVED	NAME	YEARS SERVED
Dale Arbuckle	1958-1970, 1975	Charles H. Simpson	1958, 1963-196
John Benham	1958-1960, 1962-1965	Ray Smiser	1958-1959
Jim Berry	1958-1962, 1964	Joe Dan Trigg	1958
Harold F. Bratches	1958-1966	Tom B. Wilson	1958-1963
Bill Bryan	1958-1964	L.D. Wright	1958-1964
Gene Cheatham	1958-1998	Stanton Young	1958
Shelby Cline	1958-1967	Nick Basanda	1959-1962
Allen Coles	1958-1973, 1991-1997	Frank Dolf, Jr.	1959-1970
Roy Deal	1958-1965	Glen Fowler	1959-1962
Stanley Draper, Jr.	1958-1998	W.T. "Bill" Hale	1959-1968
W.A. "Dick" Easley	1958-1970	W.C. Hamor	1959-1960
John E. Flood	1958-1987	J.W. Hunt	1959-1961
Bill Fuchs	1958-1960, 1964	Howard Lester	1959-1963
Earl W. Hall	1958-1960	Bill McVey	1959-1975
J.M. Hamilton	1958-1959	Layton Perry	1989-2002
Ralph E. Hess	1958	John Speck	1959-1960
Harold D. Hines	1958-1975	Robert Vaughn	1959-1974
Bernard Ille	1958-1964, 1981-1983	Tom Atkins	1960
Walter Kraft	1958-1960	W.J. Wallace	1960-1966
H.B. Lee	1958-1973	Robert Fullerton	1961-1987
C.F. Marsey	1958	Ben Klusmeyer	1961-1962
Thurman Medley	1958-1979, 1981	Arnold Shelley	1961-1983
Haskell Mogridge	1958-1968	James Starr	1961-1962
Jack Moncrief	1958-1999	John Thompson	1961-1968, 1974-1975
Walter A. Moore	1958	Randel Whitton, Jr.	1961-1963
R.E. "Bob" Nipp	1958-1973	Lee Allan Smith	1962-1980
W.J. O'Connor	1958-1961	Tom Tirey	1962-1964
Leon Penn	1958, 1961-1965, 1974	Jim Wade	1962
C.O. Penwell	1958-1966	Bob Bergmann	1984-Present
E.L. "Jim" Roederer	1958-1960, 1963-1966	Guy Fuller, Jr.	1963-1968
Jay Simon	1958-1959	Jack Hoberecht	1963-1975
		Joel Moore	1963-1965

NAME	YEARS SERVED	NAME	YEARS SERVED	NAME	YEARS SERVED
Jack Workman	1963-1966	Dick Champlin	1972-1988, 2007 (a)	Mike Burns	1978-1979
Art Dansereau	1964-1967	Emmit Hendrick	1972-1988	Fred Moulder	1978, 1981
John Philbin	1964-1983, 1985-Present	Doug Bell	1973-1974	Frank Murphy	1978
John E. Laughlin	1965-1966	Floyd Doolittle	1973	Art Proctor	1978
R.B. Nelson	1965-1967, 1969-1973	Frank Hill	1973-1983	Glen Schoenhals	1978-1979
Keith O'Bannon	1965-1971	Charles Lutz	1968-Present	Carrol Scott	1978
Jerry Bugg	1966-1986	Ray Arnn	1974	Don Buckalew	1979
Carl Grant	1966-1983	Keith Blair	1974-1975	Al Locke	1979-1980
Dick Medley	1966-1972	W.O. Coleman	1974-1979	Pat Downes	1979, 1981-1988, 1995
Les Metheny	1966-1970	Jack James	1974-1975	Jim Fite	1979
Brewster Hobby	1967-1968	Keith Price	1974-1992	Mike Kerran	1979-1981
Mike Miller	1967-1970	Jack Thomas	1974	Tom Mills	1979
Gary Rawlinson	1967	Glenn Boyer	1975-1988, 1991-2002	John Shelley	1979, 1981
Bud Carson	1968-1970	Mauel Heusman	1975	Doug Brant	1981-1986
Dick Mayes	1968-1974	Grant Burget	1976-1979	Tom Cheatham	1981
Don McMahon	1968-1979	Luther Holman	1976	Hal Clifford	1981
Ron Norick	1968-1971	Joe Kernke, Jr.	1976-1979	Gilbert Hyroop	1981-1982
Karl Wheland	1968	Bill Mateja	1976-1979	Tom Miller	1981, 1991-1997, 1999-Present
Bob Barton	1969-1980	Jerry Plant	1976		
Jim Pitts	1969-1992	Chet Robertson	1976	Bill Nashert	1981-2000
Gene Wright	1969	Rick Corn	1977-1988	Jim Pafford	1981-1983, 1985-1995
Bob Bunce	1970-1973	Wayne Garrison	1977-1979	Bennie Riddles	1981-1983, 1985-1996
Smokey Davidson	1970	Bob Gingrich	1977-1978	Bob Sine	1981-1983, 1985-1989
Bob Hill	1970	Mike Hickey	1977-1998	James Thielke	1981-1993
Kim Kimerling	1970-1983	Harry Jones	1977	Mike Vaughn	1981
Dave McNeill	1970-1971	Owen Martinez	1977	Mike Vervack	1981-1982
Dale Mitchell, Jr.	1970-1974	Jim Morgan	1977-1979, 1981-1990	Dale Vaughn	1982, 1999-Present
Stephen V. Payne	1970-1974	Bill Patterson	1977	Mike Bohrofen	1983-Present
Jim Richards	1970	Jamie Pitts	1977, 1979-1981	Bing Hampton	1983-1989
Larry Smith	1970-1973	Gary Rosenhamer	1977-1996	Pete Reed	1983
Bob Stipes	1970	Ken Whittington	1977-1983, 1985-Present	Gene Ritz	1983
John D. Flood	1971-1993			Linda Bancroft	1984-1985
David Moutray	1971-1975	Allan Brunett	1978	David Cleaver	1984-1987

NAME	YEARS SERVED	NAME	YEARS SERVED	NAME	YEARS SERVED
Don Douglas	1984-Present	Sam Ott	1991-Present	Gary Castro	2000
Kandy Fong	1984-1989	David Seat	1991	Mike Davenport	2000-2002
Lloyd Hardin, Jr.	1984-1987	Joe Groves	1992-Present	Steve Griffin	2000-Present
Bill Lane	1984-1986, 1988-1990	Calvin M. Johnson	1994-1995	Bill Leeper	2000-Present
Phil Stout	1984-1987	Russ Bergmann	1994-1995	Jeff Martin	2000
Bill Bumpus	1985-Present	Leo Brown	1994-1995	Mike Means	2000-2003
Kirk Hagan	1985-1994, 1996	Robbie Robertson	1994-1998	Ron Radigonda	2000
Tom Kennedy	1986	Glenn Smith, D.O.	1994-1995	Rebecca VanPool	2000
Don Linsenmeyer	1986-1989	Don Cornell	1995	Harry Wetz	2000-2002
Jack Thompson	1986-Present	Walt Gillispie	1995-Present	Ron Cunningham	2001-2004
Pete White	1986-1996	Glen Morgan	1995-Present	Rick Guererri	2001-2004
Tracy Freeny	1987-1993	Greg Price	1995-Present	Steve Hammond	2001-2002
Mark Patton	1987	Peter Bradford	1996-2000	Jim Hatfield	2001-Present
Ken Warner	1987-Present	Ben Byers	1996-Present	Barry Northcutt	2001-Present
Mark Williams	1987-Present	Rick Townsend	1996-1997	Darrell Palmer	2001-Present
Bill Bishop	1988	Kevin Akin	1997-Present	Mike Turek	2001-2002
Andy Coats	1988	Butch Freeman	1997-Present	Kenny Whittington	2001-Present
Dick Dugan	1988-Present	Greg Gawey	1997-1999	Sue Campbell	2003-Present
Leon Edd	1988	Tommy Tubbs	1997-1999	Shannon Nance	2003-Present
John Funk	1988-1992	Barry Whittington	1997-2000	Matt Bown	2004-Present
George Nigh	1988	Matt Wilson	1997	Gary Desjardins	2004-Present
Russ Stanley	1988-1991	Daniel Murdock	1998-1999	Daniel Medley	2004-Present
Jim Allred	1989-1993	Jeff Baum	1999-2000	Sandy Price	2004-Present
Steve Bugg	1989-1994	Dick Beshear	1999-Present	Brent Brewer*	2006
Steven Cagle	1989-1996	Tim Brassfield	1999-Present	Drew Dugan*	2007
Joyce Chambless	1989-1996	Dan Caldwell	1999	Mark Kelly*	2007
James Dickson	1989-1995, 2001-Present	Rob Cherry	1999-Present	Dr. Mike Kiehn*	2007
Terry McLemore	1989-1993	Jeff Cloud	1999-Present	Tony Kyle*	2007
David Mercer	1989-1991	Scott Douglas	1999-Present	James Monsees*	2007
Porter Morgan III	1989-1992	Amy Fordham	1999-2000		
D.R. Shipley	1989-2000, 2007-Present	Kevin Perry	1999-Present		
Roy L. Clymer	1991	Randy Roper	1999	*Associate	
Randa Draper	1991-1998	Greg Winters	1999-2003		

AAA ELECTRIC

A-I ELECTRIC

A-CROSS RANCH, LTD

AKIN, GARY & EDIE

ALLIED REALTORS

ALLISON INSURANCE AGENCY

ALMEN, CURT

ALWARD, CHARLES W., JR.

AMERICAN MILLWORK

ANDERSON & HOUSE

APACHE BANK

ARMSTRONG, SHARLA

ARROWHEAD ENERGY, INC.

ARTHUR, GENE

ARVEST BANK

ASKINS, JARI

ASKINS, MARTY

ASSOCIATED GLASS COMPANY

ATC FREIGHTLINER GROUP

ATLAS PAVING CO

BAILEY, DAVID

BALE CORPORATION, THE

BALL, LLOYD M.

BANCFIRST

BANK OF NICHOLS HILLS

BANK OF OKLAHOMA

BARNES, JAMES D.

BARTHOLOMEW, JAMES & TERRY

BASIN ENTERPRISES

BATCHELDER, GENE

BAUER, RAY

B. C. CLARK JEWELERS

BEALE PROFESSIONAL SERVICES

BEASLEY, DR. WILLIAM L.

BERG, TAMARA S. DENTISTRY

BERGMANN, BOB

BEVCO, INC.

BILL J. TRAUB FARMS

BLAIR, GREGORY

BLANCA, INC.

BLASER, MIKE

BLUM, WILLIAM J., DOS.

BOWN, DON

BOWN, MATT

BOYER, GLENN R.

BRADFORD-IRWIN INSURANCE

BRAGG, JEFF

BREWER CONSTRUCTION CO

BREWER, MARK

BREWER, MIKE

BRIAN QUEEN APPRAISAL CO.

BRIGGS, ROBERT

BROADWAY MEDICAL CLINIC

BURKETT, WILLIAM R.

BURTON, DEBBIE

BUTCHER, BOB

BUTTERFIELD, STEVEN B.

BYERS, BEN

BYERS, MEREDITH A.

BYRNE, PATRICK

CAGLE, STEPHEN, M.D.

CALDWELL, ROD

CAMERON, DON, JR.

CAMPBELL, SUE

CARTER, BRAD

CARY, ROY "PEE WEE"

CENTENNIAL MARKETING GROUP

CHAMPLIN, RICHARD H.

CHASTAIN, STEPHEN A., DDS

CHEAP BROTHERS INSURANCE

CHEATHAM, JAMES E., JR., M.D.

CHEF'S REQUESTED FOODS, INC.

CHEROKEE PUBLISHING CO

CHERRY, ROB

CHILES, MARVIN W.

CITIZENS BANK OF ADA

CLARK, DONALD E.

CLASSIC PRINTING

CLEEK, CHARLES H.

CLEMENTS FOODS COMPANY

CLYDE RIGGS CONSTRUCTION CO

COBBS, JIM & JAN

COGGIN, PRESTON

COHENOUR, CYNTHIA

COLE, JIM COLE & REED, PC.

COLEMAN, STEVE, PC

CONRAD-MARR DRUG #6

CONSTRUCTION BUILDING SPECIALTIES, INC.

COOK, ROD

COOLEY, RON

COOPER, JACKIE

COPPERMARK BANK

CORNER ENERGY, LLC

COURT, LEONARD

COWDEN, LESTER, III

CROOKS, CHARLES E.

CRUM, CHARLES K.

CUNNINGHAM, J. R. & KRISTY

DARNELL DRILLING

DARNOLD, SCOTT

DAVIS, BOB

DAVIS, CHUCK

DAVIS, GARY

DAVIS, JIM

DAVIS, ROBERT E. & KATHY

DEGNER, DR. CHRIS

DENISON, DOUG & DIANE

DENKER, RICK

DESJARDINS, GARY

DEVINE, MARK

DEZIGN PARTNERSHIPS, INC.

DICKSON, JAMES R.

DIFFEE MOTORS, EL RENO

DIFFEE MOTORS

DILLON, LOWELL

DITCHWITCH OF OKLAHOMA

DITCHWITCH OF TULSA

DITMARS, DR. JOHN J., JR.

DONCHIN, STEVE

DOUGLAS, SCOTT

DOWD, TIMOTHY C.

DOWNING, CRAIG

DUGAN, DICK

DUGGER, RICHARD L.

DUNCAN BUILDERS SUPPLY

DUNCAN, WILLIAM J.

DUNN, RANDALL

DURBIN LARIMORE & BIALICK

ECKART, DAVID

ECKSTEIN, TED

EDMOND DOOR & PLYWOOD

EDNEY, BOB & JEANIE

ELIAS BOOKS & BROWN

ELK CITY DAILY NEWS

ELLIOTT, IRMA B.

ELLIS, ROBERT S., M.D

EMBASSY SUITES HOTEL

EMERSON, SCOTT & ALICIA

EMSCO ELECTRIC

ENGEL LAND SERVICES, INC.

EPHRAIM, ALLAN & JAN

ESKRIDGE OLDS/LEXUS OF OKC

EVEREST, JAMES H.

FAA CREDIT UNION

FARHA, STEPHEN S.

FARHOOD, VINCENT

FARM BUREAU INSURANCE

FARMERS & MERCHANTS BANK

FERGUSON, BILL

FIFTIETH STREET SINCLAIR

FIRST BETHANY BANK & TRUST

FIRST FIDELITY BANK,

FIRST NATIONAL BANK, MWC

FIRST SECURITY BANK

FIRST UNITED BANK

FISHER, RON

FIVE G'S CONSTRUCTION

FLATT, J. B.

FLEMING, TIM

FOLGER, TERESA, M.D.

FLOWERS, BOB

FOSTER, CHARLES

FRATES, ROD

FRAZIER, KEN & MELBA

FREDERICKSON, WILLIAM A.

FREDERICKSON, DEBRA

FREEMAN, FORREST "BUTCH"

FRY, MR. & MRS DAVID E.

FULKERSON, JERRY

DRS. FUNELL & STREBEL

GABLE, JOAN

GARRETT & COMPANY

GCR TRUCK TIRE CENTER

GEO TESTING

GEIS, DONALD R.

GIBSON, MIKE

GILLISPIE & OGILBEE CPAS, INC

GIST, FRED J.

GIVENS, GREG D.

GOLD, BILL

GOODING, CLIFF & LORI

GOODWIN, MEE & FREEDE, LLP

GRAY, ANNE KRAFT

GRAY, JOE D.

GREGSTON, JAY L.

GRIFFIN, STEVE

GRIFFIN, TREY

GROTH, ROBERT W.

GROVES, JOE

GRUBE, GEORGE & CHERRI

GUSTAFSON, RICHARD

H&H MASONRY

H K & S IRON

HACKNEY, JOHN

HAFFNER, STAN

HAGAN, ALLEN

HAGAN, KIRK & KENDALL

HAHN SERVICES

HALL, FRED

HALVERSTADT, DONALD B., M.D

HAMBRICK, JOAN B.

HARLESS, GLEN M.

HARRIS, ARLYN C.

HARTZOG CONGER & CASON

HATFIELD, JAMES R.

HAVENS, JERRY

HAWKINS, LARRY

HAYES, MAGRINI & GATEWOOD, ATTORNEYS

HEATH, DON

HEATLY, CHARLES K.

HEATLY, DANNY

HENDRICK, R. B. & SONS

HICKS, ROGER & ASSOC GROUP INS.

HILL, JEFF

HILL, RANDY KING

HILL, TIMOTHY J.

HOGAN, RANDY

HOLLOMAN, JAMES H.

HOOK, DR. CARL

HOOKS, RIDGE

HOPEMAN, TODD & CHRISTINE

HORNE, B. J.

HORTON, R. H.

HOUCK INSURANCE AGENCY

HOYER CONSTRUCTION CO

HRBACEK FARMS

HULL, MIKE

HUMPHREY, JAMES

HUMPHREYS, JAY

HUTSON, HERBERT G.

ILLE, BERNIE

INGRAM, DARRYL

INSIGHT, LLC

INTEGRITY ASSET MANAGEMENT, INC.

INTERNATIONAL INSURANCE BROKERS, LTD.

INTERIOR DESIGNERS SUPPLY

J & N INVESTMENTS

JDLR ENTERPRISES

IVEN, VAN SHEA

J R D ENTERPRISES

JACKSON, DONNA, ATTORNEY

JACKSON, TRAVIS

JENSEN, JIM & JANICE

JIM WALLACE INSURANCE

JOHNSON & ASSOCIATES

JOHNSON, BETTY RODGERS

JOHNSTON & ASSOCIATES

JONES, MARTIN K., M.D.

K & K SERVICES, LLC

KALCICH, MICHAEL & JAMIE

KATES, CHRIS

KATES, KEVIN

KECKEL, PETE & KAY

KELLE OIL COMPANY

KEELE, STEVE

KEELING, BRENDA

KELLY, MARK

KELLEY, SEAN, M.D.

KEN'S BOAT SALES

KIERL, J. PETER, DDS

KILGO, SCOTT & CHERIE

KILLAM, KAREN A.

KIMBERLING, KIM

KLINGENBERG, KEN & GAILE

KLINGENBERG, RICK

KODIAK PRODUCTION CO

KREBS BREWING CO

KRITTENBRINK, DAVID J.

KROEKER, BRYAN

KYLE, TONY

LA REAU, TYLER & LESLIE

LABRIE, JOHN A.

LAKE HEFNER GOLF SHOP

LANE, RICHARD & PAM

LANIER, JERRY

LARKIN ENGINEERING

LARSEN, HANK

LAUDERDALE, MICHAEL F.

LEE, DEBORAH

LEE, RONALD

LEEMASTER, LARRY D., DDS

LEEPER, BILL

LESTER LOVING & DAVIES

LEVERICH, STEVE & CONNIE

LIBRA ELECTRIC

LIENHARD, PAUL

LINDSEY, BILL

FAMILY OF KEITH LINDUFF

LINEHAN, CAROLINE & JOHN

LINSENMEYER, DON

LIPPERT BROS, INC.

LISLE, JIM

LOCKE, AL

LONG, CHIP

LUTZ, CHARLES B., JR.

LYTLE, JEFF

ME/CU

MTCI

MACKEY, WILLIS

MAHONEY, PAT

MAROLYN PRYOR REALTORS

MARR, JAMES E.

MARRIOTT COURTYARD

MARTIN, CHADE

MARTIN, HEATH

MARTIN, SUSAN C.

MASON PIPE & SUPPLY

MAY, BOB

MCALISTER, KENNETH

MCBRIDE CLINIC

MCCLURE, BRAD

MCCORD, RON J.

MCCORMICK, DENVER

MCDONALD, STEPHEN

MCFATRIDGE INSURANCE

MCHALE, TERRY W.

MCPHERSON, KENNETH D.

MCREE, DICK & ANN

MEANS, MIKE

MEDICAL SPECIALITY SUPPLY OF
OKLAHOMA

MEDLEY, DANIEL

MEDLEY-TURRENTINE
INSURANCE

METHENY CONCRETE
PRODUCTS

METHENY, STEVEN P.

METRO ELECTRIC

MICUE, KEVIN

MID-CON DATA SERVICES

MIDLANDS MANAGEMENT
CORP

MIDWEST TROPHY CO

MIDWEST WRECKING CO

MILES, ROBERT W, M.D.

MILLER, CHRISTOPHER

MILLER, W. T. "TOM"

MINUTEMAN PRESS

MITCHELL, JOHN W, M.D.

MORAN, MICHAEL A, CPA

MORGAN, GLEN

MORGAN, JACK

MORRIS, JEFF

MORRIS, MARK

MOSER, CHARLES F.

MR. ROOTER CORP

MUTUAL ASSURANCE ADMIN.,
INC

MYERS, DANNY

NAIFEH, TODD

NEESE ENTERPRISES

PROPERTY INSURORS

PUCKETT, CHARLES W, III

PURNELL, KIRK

NORICK INVESTMENT CO

NORTHCUTT, BARRY, M.D.

NORTHCUTT, DAVE

NORTHWEST PHYSICAL
THERAPY CLINIC

NORTHWEST ROOFING

OG&E

OAKLEY, LYNDEN

OK DEVELOPMENT FINANCE
AUTHORITY

OK EMPLOYEES CREDIT UNION

OK SOCIETY OF CPA'S

OK TRANSMISSION SUPPLY

OK CITY TRACTOR

OKLAHOMA GENERAL AGENCY

OKLAHOMA TANK LINES

OK HOOPS

OMEGA ROYALTY CO, LLC

ORR, GEORGE

OSBORNE ELECTRIC COMPANY

OWEN AUTO SUPPLY

PALMER, DARREL

PARK, ALMA

PARKER, JIMMIE K, INC.

PARRISH, TEDDY

PARRISH, TIMOTHY

PAULS VALLEY TAG OFFICE

PAYNE, DAVID

PEACE, JERRY

PENNER, DWAINE

PENSION SOLUTIONS, INC.

PEPER FENCE CO, DEWEY, OK

PERRY PUBLISHING

PERRY, LAYTON

PETERS & CHANDLER CPA's

PHELPS, LYLA

PIERCE, LARRY L.

PIGG, BOBBY

PLASTER & WALD
CONSULTANTS

PLATER, D FRANK, JR.

PLUMBING SOLUTIONS

POLAND, GREGORY L., PC

POWELL, RAINEY

PRICE, JAMES R.

PRICE, SANDY

PRIVOTT, MARK B.

QUAIL CREEK BANK

QUALITY WHOLESALE
MILLWORK

RACKLEY, JACK

RACZKOWSKI, CARL, M.D.

RAMEY, GEORGE H.

R. B. AKINS COMPANY

REED, DON

REEDER, DALE B.

REEVES, ROY A.

REGIER, TODD, MD

REMPEL, VIC

RENAISSANCE HOTEL

RENTQUIK ENTERPRISES

RICHARDSON, KENNETH

RIDLING, RONNY

RITZ, JOHN

ROBERTS, PETER & KIM

ROBERTSON, JOHN D.

ROGERS, MIKE

ROGERS, TODD

ROSEBURE, BAILEY & CRAIG

ROSS, DAVID G.

ROTHWELL, DAVID, M.D.

RUDY CONSTRUCTION CO

RUFFNER, STAN

RYAN, MIKE

RYEL, TERRY

SAHMAUNT, BUD

SANFORD, CHAD

SAXON, CHARLES E.

SCHLEGEL, MARVIN K.

SCHROEDER, JIM

SCHWARZ, DOUG

SHAWVER & SON

SHIPLEY, D. R.

SHOCKLEY, JOE

SHRUM, STEVE

SILVER, JEFF

SIMPSON, MIKE

SINGER, DAVID

SKIRVIN HILTON HOTEL

SLEEM, MICHAEL A.

SLOAN, CAROL

SMITH, CARL

SMITH CARNEY & COMPANY

SMITH, CECIL C., JR.

SMITH, EDDIE CAROL

SMITH, FRED C.

SMITH, JUDGE GALE F.

SMITH, JAMES R.

SMITH, LEE ALLAN

SMITHTON, BILL & LINDA

SNODGRASS, BRAXTON

SNYDER, JOHN

SNYDER, W. A.

SOONER LEGENDS INN &
    SUITES

SOUTHWEST TRAILERS & EQUIP

SOUTHWESTERN ROOFING

SPECK PHILBIN ATTORNEY'S

SPENCE, DEAN, MD

SPENCER'S IGA, BLANCHARD

SPENCER'S IGA, PURCELL

SPICER & SANDBURG

STAFFORD, ROBERT "BOB"

STALLINGS, VERNIE

STEPHENSON, ROBERT L.

STILLWATER NATIONAL BANK

STODDART, BILL

STOUT, LOYD

STRATEGIER PLUMBING

STREBEL, GARYE, M.D.

STRELLER, SCOTT

SUMMERS, DOUGLAS G.

SUSAN, CHARLES

T&W TIRE

TATE, MIKE

TAYLOR, CLAYTON

TAYLOR, CLAYTON, JR.

THIELKE, JAMES E.

THOMPSON, DREW & BLAKE

THOMPSON, EDITH

THOMPSON, JACK

TOLBERT, JAMES R., III

TOLLETT, CHARLES A., SR., M.D.

TRAJAN DEVELOPMENT CO

TRIAD DESIGN GROUP

TRIANGLE/A & E

TRINITY BRICK SALES

TRUDGEON, JON C.T.

TUNNELL, JOE

TWENTY-TWENTY OIL & GAS

UMB BANK

UPCHURCH, DARRYL

VAN HORN, CRAIG A.

VAN METER, BOB

VERNON, PHYLLIS & RICHARD

VEST CHARLIE, M. D.

VEST, JACQUIE

VISION BANK, ADA

W W LIVESTOCK CORP.

WADE, GARY

WAGNER, PAUL R.

WALSH, THOMAS B., CPA

WARNER, KEN

WARWICK ANIMAL HOSPITAL

WEBB, TOM R.

WEDGEWOOD PET CLINIC

WESTPHALEN, GARY

WHETSEL, SHERIFF JOHN

WHITE, DENNIS

WHITENECK, DR. SUSAN

WHITTINGTON, KEN D.

WHITTINGTON, KENNETH W., M.D.

WILKS, JONATHAN

WILLIAMS, C. MARK

WILLIAMS, JERRY L., CPA

WILLIAMS, JOHN K. & BEVERLY

WILLIAMS, KEVIN

WILSON, TOM

WINN, JIM

WIPFLI, GERALD

WIPFLI, JEFF, M.D.

WOODSON, DOUGLAS, DDS

WYANT, DEBBIE

WYSKUP, ROBERT J.

YATES, CARLAN, M.D.

YATES, GAYLAN, M.D.

YOUNG ENERGY, INC.

YOUNG, TONY

YUKON NATIONAL BANK

ZIESE, CARL H.

MAJOR ACCOMPLISHMENTS OF THE ALL SPORTS ASSOCIATION

In 2007, Oklahoma City All Sports Association is proud to celebrate its 50th Anniversary.
Originally created in 1957 to support and maintain the All–College Basketball Tournament, accomplishments have
expanded to more than 220 events in Oklahoma City, including 30 NCAA Championships since 1983.

• 1957

TWENTY-SECOND ANNUAL ALL-COLLEGE TOURNAMENT
– MUNICIPAL AUDITORIUM
First time for ASA, a newly-established organization, to host the All-College.

BIG 4 DOUBLE HEADER
OU vs. Tulsa; OSU vs. OCU

• 1958

"CELEBRITY" SOFTBALL GAME CO-SPONSORED WITH OKC AMATEUR BASEBALL ASSOCIATION
Featherheaded Greenies vs. Mudville Sluggers

NATIONAL INDUSTRIAL LEAGUE GAMES
Phillips 66ers vs. Peoria Caterpillars and Wichita Vickers

POST SEASON TOUR STOP OF THE TOP 20 NBA STARS

FIRST HIGH SCHOOL FOOTBALL PREP PREVIEW
– TAFT STADIUM
Eleven teams played and the program raised $150,000 for high schools over a 12-year period. (Also, 1958-1970)

• 1959

PROFESSIONAL FOOTBALL GAME
– OWEN FIELD
Detroit Lions vs Philadelphia Eagles

NBA EXHIBITION
– MUNICIPAL AUDITORIUM
St. Louis Hawks vs. Cincinnati Royals

• 1961

FIRST ALL SPORTS BOWL GAME FOR JUNIOR COLLEGES
– TAFT STADIUM
Langston vs. Panhandle

• 1962

NEW BASEBALL FACILITY ON THE FAIRGROUNDS NAMED ALL SPORTS STADIUM BY ACTION OF THE CITY COUNCIL

• 1964

OKC ALL SPORTS ARRANGES COMMITMENT FROM THE LONE STAR CONFERENCE AND OKLAHOMA COLLEGIATE CONFERENCE TO PROVIDE RIVAL TEAMS FOR THE ALL SPORTS BOWL.

• 1968

WORLD SOFTBALL TOURNAMENT
– ALL SPORTS STADIUM
Teams from 11 countries participated.

• 1972

BIG FOUR DOUBLEHEADER
OCU vs. OU; OSU vs. TU
One of the first events at the new Myriad

• 1973

GENERAL ASSEMBLY OF THE INTERNATIONAL SPORTS FEDERATION
– MYRIAD.
First time held outside of Europe

• 1974

U.S. OPEN TABLE TENNIS TOURNAMENT
– MYRIAD

• 1976

AMERICAN BOWLING CONGRESS TOURNAMENT
– MYRIAD

•1977

NCAA MEN'S DIVISION I BASKETBALL SUB REGIONAL/1ST AND 2ND ROUNDS
– MYRIAD
(Also 1977, 1994, 1998, 2003, 2005)

FIRST OKC ALL SPORTS MEMBERSHIP DRIVE
– 743 memberships sold

• 1978

FIRST BIG EIGHT CONFERENCE BASEBALL CHAMPIONSHIP
– ALL SPORTS STADIUM.
(Also 1976-1996)

• 1982

SOONER STATE GAMES BEGIN.
(Adopted by ASA, 1989-2007)

• 1983

FIRST NCAA DIVISION I WRESTLING CHAMPIONSHIP
– MYRIAD
First time held outside a college campus.
(Also 1983, 1985, 1989, 1992, 2006)

• 1984

OKC ALL SPORTS NEGOTIATES TO BE A HOST TO 1989 NATIONAL OLYMPIC SPORTS FESTIVAL.

• 1985

NCAA DIVISION I WOMEN'S TENNIS CHAMPIONSHIP
– MYRIAD

FIFTIETH ANNUAL ALL-COLLEGE BASKETBALL TOURNAMENT
– MYRIAD.
OSU, SMU, OU, Cincinnati

• 1986

FIRST NCAA MEN'S AND WOMEN'S INDOOR TRACK AND FIELD CHAMPIONSHIP
– MYRIAD
(Also 1986-1987)

• **1988**

OKC ALL SPORTS ESTABLISHES OPERATION
AND OFFICE INDEPENDENT OF OKC
CHAMBER OF COMMERCE.

• **1989**

BMX GRAND NATIONALS
– MYRIAD
(Also 1988-1997)

NATIONAL BASKETBALL COACHES GOLF
INVITATIONAL
– OAK TREE

Bicycle moto-xcross racers jump
for the lead. The ASA hosted
the BMX Grand Nationals
at the Myriad for nine years.
With nearly 4,000 contestants
representing all 50 states, the
event brought more than 10,000
visitors to Oklahoma City each
year. *Courtesy Oklahoma City All
Sports Association.*

• **1990**

FIRST AEROSPACE AMERICA
– WILL ROGERS WORLD AIRPORT
(Also 1990-1997)

FIRST INTERNATIONAL FINALS RODEO
– MYRIAD
(Also 1990-1995)

FIRST NCAA WOMEN'S COLLEGE SOFTBALL
WORLD SERIES
– ASA HALL OF FAME STADIUM
Total attendance 11,938
(Also 1990-1995, 1997-2007)

• **1994**

RUSSIAN HOCKEY TEAM EXHIBITION
– MYRIAD
vs. OKC Blazers

• **1995**

BIG EIGHT WOMEN'S TENNIS
CHAMPIONSHIP
– OKC TENNIS CENTER.
A record attendance of 4,911.

FIRST BIG 12 SOFTBALL CHAMPIONSHIP
– ASA HALL OF FAME STADIUM
(Also 1995-2007)

• **1997**

FIRST BIG 12 BASEBALL CHAMPIONSHIP
– ALL SPORTS STADIUM
(Also 1997- 2001, 2003, 2005-2007)

• **1998**

FIRST ALL SPORTS GOLF INVITATIONAL
– JIMMIE AUSTIN OU GOLF COURSE
(Also 1998-2007)

• **2001**

TOUCHSTONE ENERGY BECOMES THE
FIRST TITLE SPONSOR OF THE ALL-COLLEGE
CLASSIC.

ABE LEMONS AWARD ESTABLISHED TO RECOGNIZE ALL-COLLEGE TOURNAMENT COACHES AND NATION'S TOP 3-POINT SHOOTER.

• **2002**

OKC ALL SPORTS BEGINS A THREE YEAR ALL-COLLEGE BASKETBALL CLASSIC PARTNERSHIP AGREEMENT WITH ESPN.
First time for national TV exposure.

• **2003**

FIRST ALL SPORTS BASKETBALL ADVENTURE HELD IN CONJUNCTION WITH THE ALL-COLLEGE CLASSIC
– COX BUSINESS SERVICES CENTER.
(Also 2003-2007)

• **2004**

OKC ALL SPORTS HOSTS THE MCDONALD'S HIGH SCHOOL ALL-AMERICAN GAMES.
– FORD CENTER

OKC ALL SPORTS ESTABLISHES A SCHOLARSHIP PROGRAM AWARDING $1,000 SCHOLARSHIPS TO HIGH SCHOOL SENIORS.

• **2005**

O'REILLY AUTO PARTS BECOMES TITLE SPONSOR OF 70TH ALL-COLLEGE CLASSIC.

• **2006**

THE NCAA WRESTLING CHAMPIONSHIPS ACHIEVES THE 2ND HIGHEST ATTENDANCE RECORD FOR THE CHAMPIONSHIP.
– FORD CENTER

THE NCAA WOMEN'S COLLEGE WORLD SERIES BREAKS ATTENDANCE RECORD WITH 46,122. EVERY GAME IS TELEVISED LIVE FOR THE FIRST TIME ON ESPN.
– ASA HALL OF FAME STADIUM

OKC ALL SPORTS ACHIEVES STATUS FOR OKLAHOMA CITY AS "HOME OF THE BIG 12 CONFERENCE BASEBALL CHAMPIONSHIP" FROM THE CONFERENCE.

• **2007**

FIRST PHILLIPS 66 BIG 12 MEN'S & WOMEN'S BASKETBALL CHAMPIONSHIPS
– FORD CENTER & COX CONVENTION CENTER

THE NCAA WOMEN'S COLLEGE WORLD SERIES BREAKS ATTENDANCE RECORD WITH 62,463.

Events hosted by the OKC All Sports Association benefit Oklahoma City by providing quality athletic competition, family entertainment options and a boost to the city's economy. At the same time, the events garner widespread attention and attract visitors from around the globe to Oklahoma City.

OPPOSITE: 2007 Big Twelve Women's Championship final game action in the Cox Convention Center Arena. Sports columnist Barry Tramel had this to say about the primary venue for ASA events over the years: "…the star of the historic first day of Oklahoma City's Big 12 tournament adventure was a 35 year old lady who doesn't even know her name. If its' OK with you, lets call her the Myriad. The downtown arena, far removed from its heyday as a sports coliseum, sparkled again Tuesday. The place glistened like Christmas: you would have sworn this was *That 70s Show*, and that Kresimir Cosic was in town for the All-College, or Al McGuire for the NCAA regionals."
Courtesy Oklahoma City All Sports Association.